mustsees
London

Riccardo Sala / age fotostock

mustsees **London**

Editorial Director	Cynthia Clayton Ochterbeck
Edited & Produced by	Jonathan P. Gilbert, Azalay Media
Contributing Writer	Helen Ochyra
Production Manager	Natasha G. George
Cartography	Stephane Anton, John Dear, Thierry Lemasson
Layout	Natasha G. George
Interior Design	Chris Bell, cbdesign
Cover Design	Chris Bell, cbdesign, Natasha G. George
Contact Us	Michelin Travel and Lifestyle North America
	One Parkway South
	Greenville, SC 29615
	USA
	travel.lifestyle@us.michelin.com
	www.michelintravel.com
	Michelin Travel Partner
	Hannay House
	39 Clarendon Road
	Watford, Herts WD17 1JA
	UK
	✆01923 205240
	travelpubsales@uk.michelin.com
	www.ViaMichelin.com
Special Sales	For information regarding bulk sales,
	customized editions and premium sales,
	please contact us at:
	travel.lifestyle@us.michelin.com
	www.michelintravel.com

Michelin Travel Partner
Société par actions simplifiées au capital de 11 288 880 EUR
27 cours de l'Île Seguin - 92100 Boulogne Billancourt (France)
R.C.S. Nanterre 433 677 721

© Michelin Travel Partner
ISBN 978-2-067197-38-1
Printed: July 2014
Printed and bound in Italy

MIX
Paper from
responsible sources
FSC® C015829
www.fsc.org

Note to the reader:
While every effort is made to ensure that all information printed in this guide is correct
and up-to-date, Michelin Travel Partner accepts no liability for any direct, indirect or
consequential losses howsoever caused so far as such can be excluded by law. Admission
prices listed for sights in this guide are for a single adult, unless otherwise specified.

Welcome to London

Southbank and River Thames

p22

British Tourist Authority

Introduction

p78

Damir Fabijanc/Londononview

TABLE OF CONTENTS

Must Do

Must Eat

Must Stay

Must Know

p92

Ingrid Rasmussen/British Tourist Authority

TABLE OF CONTENTS

★★★ ATTRACTIONS

Unmissable historic and cultural sights

Visit Britain

Tower of London   p 73

VisitBritain / Britain on View

Westminster Abbey   p 28

© The Royal Parks

Regent's Park   p 90

Museum of London

Museum of London   p 83

Horse Guards Parade p 108

Victoria and Albert Museum p 81

Royal Botanic Gardens, Kew p 91

©Eur/World Pictures/Photoshot

Victoria and Albert Museum

Pawel Libera/Visit London

National Maritime Museum   p 79

©National Maritime Museum

St Paul's Cathedral   p 40

©Peter Smith/St Paul's Cathedral

Imperial War Museum   p 79

©Imperial War Museum

St George's Chapel, Windsor Castle   p 74

©Philip Coblentz/Brand X Pictures

ACTIVITIES

Unmissable activities and entertainment

©Ritz Hotel London

Tea at the Ritz p 141

©Kalpesh Lathigra/www.southbanklondon.com

Riverside Walk p 57

www.southbanklondon.com

Trip on the London Eye p 111

©John Tramper/Shakespeare's Globe

Shakespeare's Globe p 114

www.chinatownlondon.org

Restaurants in Chinatown p 37

STAR ATTRACTIONS

STAR ATTRACTIONS

Unmissable historic, cultural, and natural sights

For more than 75 years people have used Michelin stars to take the guesswork out of travel. Our star-rating system helps you make the best decision on where to go, what to do, and what to see.

★★★	Unmissable
★★	Worth a trip
★	Worth a detour
No star	recommended

ACTIVITIES

STAR ATTRACTIONS

CALENDAR OF EVENTS

Listed below are some of the most popular annual events. For specific dates and full details, consult the Tourist Information Centre's website www.visitlondon.com.

January
New Year's Day Parade
Piccadilly to Parliament Square
Boat Show
ExCeL Exhibition Centre
(starts first Thu)
Chinese New Year
Soho *(Jan/Feb)*

February
RBS 6 Nations Championship
(Rugby Union) Twickenham
Clowns' Church Service
Holy Trinity, Dalston *(first Sun)*
Great Spitalfields Pancake Race
(Shrove Tue)

March
Chelsea Antiques Fair
Old Town Hall, Chelsea
Head of the River Race
Thames: Mortlake to Putney
Oxford & Cambridge Boat Race
Thames: Putney to Mortlake
Ideal Home Show
Earls Court Exhibition Centre
St Patrick's Day Parade
Hyde Park to Trafalgar Square

Easter
Service and distribution of Hot Cross buns
St Bartholomew-the-Great
(Good Fri)
Easter Parade
Battersea Park *(Easter Sun)*

April
RHS Great London Plant Fair
Westminster
London Marathon
Docklands to Westminster

Feast of St George
Trafalgar Square

May
Royal Windsor Horse Show
Windsor Castle
Chelsea Flower Show
Royal Hospital, Chelsea
FA Cup Final
Wembley Stadium
Chelsea Pensioners' Oak
Apple Day Parade
Royal Hospital, Chelsea
Covent Garden May Fayre and Puppet Festival

June
Beating Retreat
Horse Guards Parade, Whitehall
Trooping the Colour
Horse Guards Parade
(Queen's Birthday)
Hampton Court Music Festival
Hampton Court Palace
Summer Music Festival
Spitalfields
AEGON Grass Court Tennis Championships
Queen's Club, West Kensington
Royal Ascot
Taste of London
Regent's Park
British Polo Open Championships
Cowdray Park
Royal Academy Summer Exhibition
Burlington House, Piccadilly
(runs until Aug)
Wimbledon Championships
All England Club, Wimbledon
(runs into July)

MUST KNOW

City of London Festival
Celebrated in the City
(runs into July)
Pride Parade
Baker Street to Trafalgar Square

July
**Hampton Court Palace
Flower Show
Sir Henry Wood's Promenade
Concerts (The Proms)**
Royal Albert Hall *(8 weeks)*
Swan Upping
River Thames
Doggett's Coat and Badge Race
London Bridge to Cadogan Pier
(Chelsea)

August
Great British Beer Festival
Olympia Exhibition Hall
London Mela
Asian arts and culture festival
Notting Hill Carnival
Ladbroke Grove
(Bank Holiday weekend)

September
**Pearly Kings and Queens
Harvest Festival**
Guildhall
Great River Race
Docklands to Ham
Mayor's Thames Festival
South Bank
**Open House London
London Fashion Week
London Design Festival**

October
Goldsmith's Show
Goldsmiths Hall *(first week)*
**Opening of the
Michaelmas Law Term**
Temple Bar to Westminster Abbey
Frieze Art Fair
Regent's Park
Halloween

August: Notting Hill Carnival

Jon Spaull/British Tourist Authority

⚓ Notting Hill Carnival
Revelers throng the streets on
the last weekend in August for
Europe's premier carnival.
⊖*Some stations close or
have restricted access on
carnival days, check website
for details. www.thenotting
hillcarnival.com.*

November
**Bonfire Night
London to Brighton
Veteran Car Run**
Departs from Hyde Park
Corner *(first Sun)*
**BFI London Film Festival
Lord Mayor's Show**
City of London
(Sat nearest to Nov 9)
Remembrance Sunday
Cenotaph, Whitehall
(11am; Sun nearest to Nov 11)
State Opening of Parliament
By the Queen at Westminster
Switching on Christmas lights
Regent Street

December
Lighting of the Christmas Tree
Trafalgar Square
Carol Services
Throughout London's churches

13

PRACTICAL INFORMATION

WHEN TO GO

London is an all-year-round, all-weather city and there are plenty of things to do and see whatever the season. **Winter** is a good time to visit many of the city's sights as they are generally less crowded, and in December shop windows are full of colorful displays and bright Christmas lights. By the time **spring** arrives, people are spending more time outdoors and even sitting at pavement cafés—though often still buttoned up in coats and scarves! The **summer** season is marked by events such as the Wimbledon Tennis Championships and the Notting Hill Carnival, and you can see open-air concerts and plays, weather permitting. **Fall** is a good time to visit London's parks and gardens when the leaves are turning color and the weather can be very pleasant and warm well into October. The city is always busier in school vacations; the main ones are at Easter, during July and August, and at Christmas, and there are mid-term breaks in February, May, and October.

KNOW BEFORE YOU GO

A little homework before you depart will help you get the most out of your trip.

Useful websites

www.visitlondon.com – Official tourist office website, with full details of events and sightseeing.
www.standard.co.uk – Website of London's free Evening Standard newspaper, with city news and entertainment listings.
www.timeout.com/london – Comprehensive entertainment listings.
www.londontown.com – Sightseeing, entertainment, services, shopping etc.
www.officiallondontheatre.co.uk – Theatre listings site run by the theatre companies themselves.

Tourist information

City of London Information Centre – St Paul's Churchyard, EC4M 8BX. The only officially recognised Tourist Information Centre in central London.

International visitors

Australian High Commission: 020 7379 4334. www.australia.org.uk.
Canadian High Commission: 020 7258 6600. www.canada.org.uk
Embassy of Ireland: 020 7235 2171. www.embassyofireland.co.uk.
New Zealand High Commission: 020 7930 8422. www.nzembassy.com.
South African High Commission: 020 7451 7299. www.southafricahouse.com.
United States Embassy: 020 7499 9000. www.usembassy.org.uk.

Entry requirements

Passports – EU nationals only need valid ID, such as a photocard driving license, to enter the UK, although it is advisable to carry a passport too. Non-EU nationals must have a passport and may need a visa. Loss or theft should be reported to the appropriate

London average seasonal temperatures			
	Jan	**Apr**	**Jul**	**Oct**
Avg. High	6°C/43°F	14°C/57°F	24°C/75°F	14°C/57°F
Avg. Low	1°C/33°F	6°C/43°F	14°C/57°F	8°C/46°F

embassy or consulate and to the local police.

Visas – Not required by nationals of the member states of the European Economic Area (EEA), the Commonwealth (including Australia, Canada, New Zealand, and South Africa), and the USA (for long stays see below). Nationals of other countries should check with the British Embassy and apply for a visa if necessary in good time. Entry visas are required by Australian, New Zealand, Canadian, and US nationals for a stay exceeding 3 months. All visitors from outside the EEA must apply for a visa before traveling if they are planning to stay for more than 6 months.

For up-to-date information on visas: www.ukvisas.gov.uk.

US citizens (travel.state.gov) for general information on visa requirements, customs regulations, medical care etc.

UK customs

EU legislation governs tax-free allowances for bringing goods into the UK, except in the Channel Islands and the Isle of Man, which have different regulations. Details are available at most ports of entry to Great Britain.

Pets – Domestic animals (dogs, cats) with vaccination documents are allowed into the UK, but the legislation is complex and animals may require a period of quarantine. Take advice several months in advance of traveling if you wish to bring animals to the UK.

GETTING THERE
By Air

London is served by five major airports — Heathrow, Gatwick, Luton, Stansted, and London City. See the London Tourist Board website (www.visitlondon.com) for details on how to get to and from the airports and central London, and on fares and timing.

Heathrow – 0844 335 1801. www.heathrowairport.com. 20mi/32km west of London off the A4/M4.

Gatwick – 0844 892 0322. www.gatwickairport.com. 30mi/48km south of London down the M25/M23.

Stansted – 0844 335 1803. www.stanstedairport.com. In Bishop's Stortford, Essex, about 34mi/54km northeast of London.

Luton – 0158 240 5100. www.london-luton.co.uk. In Luton, Bedfordshire, 32mi/51km north of London.

City Airport – 020 7646 0088. www.londoncityairport.com. The closest of the airports at 6 mi/9.6km east of central London.

By Ferry

There are numerous cross-Channel (passenger and car ferries, hovercraft) services from the Continent, the Channel Islands, and Ireland. The closest to London are the Channel ports in the east –

Dover, Folkestone, Newhaven. The Channel ports located farther west are Portsmouth, Bournemouth, Weymouth, and Plymouth. For advice on getting to and from ferry ports: www.visitlondon.com.

By Train

London has 13 mainline terminals connected by the Underground and buses. Tickets are available at train stations and can be expensive, but long-distance tickets are cheaper if you travel off-peak and book in advance. Timetable information and tickets are also available online via websites such as www.thetrainline.com and www.mytrainticket.co.uk. **Disabled travelers** should check facilities and arrange assistance at stations in advance; smaller British stations may not be particularly wheelchair-friendly. Many Underground stations are now step-free, check the tube map for the wheelchair symbol.

National Rail Enquiries – 08457 48 49 50. www.nationalrail.co.uk.

Eurostar trains from Calais, Brussels, Lille, and Paris arrive at the smart purpose-built terminal St Pancras International *(020 7843 7688)*. Eurostar: 08705 186 186; 01233 617 575 from outside the UK. www.eurostar.com.

Eurotunnel run shuttle services for vehicles through the Channel Tunnel from Calais, France to Folkestone, Kent. 0844 335 3535/0844 463 0000 *(free 24hr information service)*. www.eurotunnel.com.

By Bus

Most buses arrive at **Victoria Coach Station** in Buckingham Palace Road, 5min walk from Victoria Railway Station for rail and and Underground connections.

By Car

Most visitors traveling to London by car enter the UK through the Channel ports *(see By Ferry)*. You need the vehicle's registration papers (log-book) and a nationality plate displayed on your car. Insurance cover is compulsory; the International Insurance Certificate (Green Card), though no longer a legal requirement, is the most effective proof of insurance cover and is internationally recognized by the authorities.

GETTING AROUND

London may be a big sprawling city, but its comprehensive transport network makes it easy to get around. However, with a population numbering some 8 million, the system is bound to get a little overloaded and rush hour *(Mon–Fri 7–10am, 5–7pm)* is best avoided. See Transport for London's website for information, routes, timetables, and fares for all forms of travel: www.tfl.gov.uk.

By Bus

London's iconic red buses provide an economical and efficient way of exploring the capital. For a more lofty perspective, travel upstairs on a double decker and try and get one of the front seats if possible. White signs with the red logo indicate bus stops at which all listed buses must stop; red signs with the white logo are request stops at which passengers must wave to indicate that the bus should stop. Reduced services on some routes operate through the night. **Night buses** (prefixed with "N" or on a blue tile located on the bus stop) stop only if requested. Buses are cheaper than trains or the Underground, but they are also slower. You must have a ticket before you board. Use the ticket machines located at every bus stop (tickets cost £2.40 for a single journey of any length and you must pay again if you change buses during your journey) to buy with cash, or purchase a travelcard or Oyster card in advance. *See Ticket Options* for more details.

There are also several companies offering hop-on, hop-off **Bus Tours** of the capital:
The Original Tour:
www.theoriginaltour.com
Big Bus Tours:
www.bigbustours.com

By Rail
Docklands Light Railway (DLR) – This operates across East London, from Bank, Tower Gateway and Stratford International. Services are reduced at weekends. DLR trains are fully wheelchair-accessible. Tickets must be bought before boarding from stations.
Overground trains – See www.tfl. gov.uk for a map of the network and timetables. Tickets must be bought at the stations before boarding. *See Tickets Options.*

By Underground (Tube)
The network is divided into six zones with Zone 1 covering central London. *See map p159.* If you buy single tickets, available only at Underground stations, the Tube can

be very expensive – a single journey is £4.70 within Zone 1 – but Oyster tickets and travelcards can work out to be good value. Keep your ticket safe as you will need it to exit through the electronic barrier at the end of your journey. *See Ticket Options.*

By Taxi
Black cabs – Traditional London cabs can be hired at mainline railway stations, many Underground and bus stations, Heathrow airport, taxi ranks, and when they are cruising the streets with the orange roof-light lit up. There are normally plenty around, although they become more elusive when it's raining and at around 10.30–11pm when people are leaving the theaters and pubs. All licensed cabs are accessible to people using wheelchairs.
All black cabs are metered. The minimum fare is £2.40. Fares are higher at night *(8pm–6am)* Mon–Fri, at weekends, and on public holidays, and depend on the distance traveled and the taxi speed. Some cabs accept credit or debit cards. Check with the driver before you travel. There is an extra charge of £1 or 12.50% of the fare, whichever is higher. Tipping is discretionary but usual, around 10%. For information: www.tfl.gov.uk. To call a cab: 08700 802 902, 0700 596 3535, www.london-taxi.co.uk; 020 7253 5000, 020 7426 3420, www.dial-a-cab.co.uk.
Minicabs – Outside the city center, there are also many local licensed minicab companies, which are booked by phone *(see www.tfl. gov.uk)* and offer flat-fee journeys. They are usually cheaper than black cabs but it's a good idea to ask the

price when booking. Never use the unlicensed minicabs that cruise the city at night; if a minicab cannot be booked by phone or in an office it is illegal; many have no meter. At best you are uninsured, at worst in danger, especially lone females. For information: www.tfl.gov.uk. For the numbers of one black cab and two licensed minicab firms in the area you are texting from, text CAB to 60835 —there's a small charge for this service.

Ticket options
Multitrip passes allowing you to hop on and off as many times as you like during a certain period offer the best value for money. If you're not sure which to buy ask advice at a ticket office, or see www.visitlondon.com or http://visitorshop.tfl.gov.uk/english/ticket-types.htm.

Oyster cards – A "smartcard" storing credit. It calculates automatically the cheapest fare for all the journeys you make during a 24hr period *(4.30am–4.30am)*. Peak hours are Mon–Fri 6.30am–9.30am and 4–7pm. As an example, for travel in Zones 1–2 an adult won't pay more than £8.40 per day with an Oyster card or £7 if traveling off-peak. It can be used on the Underground, buses, most National Rail services in London *(see www.tfl.gov.uk for restrictions)*, trams, the DLR, and provide discounted travel on Thames Clipper riverboats. Make sure you touch in and out against the yellow card reader.
Travelcards – Paper tickets available for 1 or 7 days, 1 month, and a year of travel in London, and in various combinations of Zones and for peak or off-peak travel.

They can also be loaded onto your Oyster card. They can be used on the Underground, buses, most National Rail services in London *(see www.tfl.gov.uk for restrictions)*, trams, the DLR, and some Thames Clipper services.
Children's tickets – Ticket options for children are also varied but they travel free under 10 if accompanied by an adult with a valid ticket (up to 4 children per adult). Those aged 11–17 years need a photocard to obtain reduced fares (or for 11–15 years to travel free on buses and trams), which can be bought at a station or online at www.tfl.gov.uk. Information on fares by age group is also available on the site. Make sure they come armed with a passport-sized photo and birth certificate, or their passport.

By Boat
Make use of the Thames to get around London and enjoy a boat ride at the same time. Commuter services are available on several routes (see *www.thamesclippers.com*). Adult single fares start at £3.90. Holders of Travelcards and Oyster cards are entitled to a discount on some services. Tickets can be bought at the piers or on board some services. Many of the boats offer excellent guided sightseeing tours, either upstream to Kew and Hampton Court, or down the river to Greenwich.

By Bike
Transport for London's Cycle Superhighways have made it even easier to get into the city by bike, with bright blue cycle lanes running from the suburbs into the city centre. In central London, the Barclays Cycle Hire scheme offers

bikes for hire from £1 an hour (plus a daily £2 access fee) and plenty of docking stations to choose from. Minor routes are covered by the London Cycle Network. For maps and journey planning, visit www.tfl.gov.uk. London traffic is unpredictable and drivers can be impatient; wearing a safety helmet is therefore highly recommended. Bikes may be taken on some train lines at certain times (generally not during the rush hour), but you can normally take a folding bike on all forms of transport without restriction (at the driver's discretion on buses, and in containers on the DLR).

By Car

Try to avoid driving in London; traffic is dense, parking is expensive, and a £10 **congestion charge** is payable per day for entering the central zone. If you want to drive, make sure you are insured and have a valid driving license with you. For the onlne version of the **Highway Code**— the UK drivers' rulebook—go to www.direct.gov.uk. For additional information and advice see www.tfl.gov.uk/roadusers/default.aspx. Major UK motoring organizations:
Automobile Association (AA) – 0906 88 84322 *(24hr travel information)*. www.theaa.co.uk.
Royal Automobile Club (RAC) – www.rac.co.uk.

BASIC INFORMATION
Accessibility

Disabled access in hotels, attractions, and entertainment venues across London is improving, gradually: www.visitlondon.com; wwwtfl.gov.uk. To find accessible art and entertainment venues,

Oyster cards

Visitors can buy Oyster cards and Travelcards on arrival or in advance. See www.visitlondon.com/travel/oyster for more details.
Visitor Oyster cards are available for £18 (including £15 credit preloaded). Cards can also be bought and topped up with credit at Underground stations, DLR stations, London Travel Information Centres, and Oyster Ticket Stops. UK residents can also register their Oyster card online and top up through the website.

but also toilets, hotels etc: www.artsline.co.uk. RADAR publishes a guide to accommodation and transport: 020 7250 3222, www.radar.org.uk.

Accommodations

London has a range of places to stay, from hostels to hotels, with guesthouses and bed & breakfasts somewhere in between. These last two are reasonably interchangeable in terms of size and facilities. See *Must Stay* for a list of suggested hotels.

Reservations services
Hotels

♦ London Tourist Board booking service: 0870 1566 366. www.visitlondon.com/accommodation/.
♦ British Hotel Reservation Centre: 020 7592 3055. www.bhrc.co.uk.

Bed and breakfast

♦ 020 8748 1943. www.athomeinlondon.co.uk.

- 020 8769 3500.
  www.londonhometohome.com.
- 020 7586 2768.
  www.londonbb.com.
- 020 7937 2001.
  www.uptownres.co.uk.

Youth hostels
- 01629 592 629, 01629 592 700.
  www.yha.org.uk.

Academic residences
Available during vacations, they offer cheaper options.
- 0114 249 3090.
  www.venuemasters.co.uk.

Business hours
Banks are generally open Mon–Fri 9/9.30am–4.30/5pm; some are open Sat 9.30am–12.30/3.30pm; almost all banks are closed on Sun and bank holidays *(see Public Holidays)*.
Post offices open Mon–Fri 8.30/9am–5.30pm, and some open weekends too.
Stores are usually open Mon–Sat 9/10am–5.30/6pm and Sun 11am/noon–5/6pm. Some are also open evenings, especially in central London and shopping malls.

Communications
Cell phone networks in the UK use the European-standard GSM networks. US and Canadian visitors will need a tri-band phone. Since the advent of cell phones there are fewer public pay phones—if you do find one it will accept either coins, a credit card, or a British Telecom phonecard (available from post offices and some newsagents).
Area codes – To make an international call dial 00 + country code + area code (without the initial 0) + subscriber's number.

Important phone numbers	
Emergency *(24hr)* for **Fire, Police, Ambulance, Coastguard, Mountain Rescue, or Cave Rescue.**	✆ 999
Operator	✆ 100
Directory Enquiries within the UK	✆ 118 500

The area code for London is 020. Many newsagents sell **pre-pay phone cards** that offer cheap international call rates (from 2p a minute to the US); ask the shop assistant or scan the posters to find the best for your destination.

Discounts
Compared with the rest of the UK and other European cities, London is expensive, owing in particular to high living costs and transport. Discounts for the over 60s are available at many attractions and entertainment venues. Check www.tfl.gov.uk for the discount deals sometimes offered for sightseeing—from 2-for-1 on the London Eye to 30% off tickets for West End shows on presenting a valid transport ticket or Oyster card.

Electricity
The electric current is 220–240 volts AC; three-pin flat wall sockets are standard. An adaptor or multiple-point plug is required for non-British appliances, and some American 110-volt appliances will also need a transformer.

Health
Make sure you have adequate insurance. Emergency treatment via the NHS (National Health

MUST KNOW

Service) is generally free for overseas visitors, though routine treatment will need to be paid for, except for nationals from an EEA country where there is a reciprocal agreement. www.visitlondon.com/travel/medical-services.

Pharmacists (chemists) can offer advice on minor ailments and are open during business hours; some are also open late night. NHS Walk-in Centres offer advice and treatment for minor injuries and illnesses. You can also phone the NHS for medical advice *(24hr)* by dialling 111 from any phone. Both are staffed by experienced nurses. To find the nearest doctor, dentist or pharmacist: www.nhs.uk.

Internet
Free wifi is now available in many bars, cafés, hotels and restaurants. There is also wifi at most Underground stations (for a fee). To find an Internet café: www.londononline.co.uk/Cybercafes.

Money and currency exchange
The decimal system (100 pence = £1). Notes £50, £20, £10, and £5; silver coins: £2, £1, 50p, 20p, 10p, 5p (silver coins); copper coins 2p and 1p. The main credit cards are widely accepted. ID is required when cashing traveler's checks or Eurocheques. Most banks have 24hr cash dispensers (ATMs) that accept international credit cards or some debit cards, such as Maestro; these "hole in the wall" dispensers are widely available. Exchange facilities outside banking hours are available at airports, bureaux de change, travel agencies, and hotels. Report any loss or theft to the police who will issue a crime

number for use by the insurance or credit card company. *See also Business Hours.*

Post offices
See Business Hours. You can also buy stamps from selected shops, e.g. newsagents, although they stock a limited range and generally not for mailing abroad.

Public holidays
New Year's Day *(Jan 1)*; Good Friday *(Fri before Easter)*; Easter Monday *(Mon after Easter)*; May Day *(first Mon in May)*; Spring Bank Holiday *(last Mon in May)*; August Bank Holiday *(last Mon in Aug)*; Christmas Day *(Dec 25)*; Boxing Day *(Dec 26)*.

Smoking
Smoking inside public places, including bars, clubs, restaurants, and pubs is banned throughout England.

Taxes and tipping
A sales tax of 20 percent (called VAT) is added to most retail goods and services. Non-EU nationals may reclaim this tax when leaving the country; paperwork should be completed by the retailer at time of purchase.
A service charge is sometimes added to a restaurant bill automatically but you can tip in addition for great service. If no charge has been added, tip 10–12.5%. Tip taxi drivers 10% and hotel porters £1 per bag.

WELCOME TO LONDON

One of the world's preeminent metropolitan areas, London itself is divided into 32 boroughs, each with its own character. Renowned for its multicultural outlook, you can hear over 300 languages and a whole host of different accents spoken on its streets. As the UK's capital and host of four UNESCO World Heritage Sites, London's sights, sounds, and attractions have something to seduce every visitor.

From its beginnings as Londinium, founded by the Romans, the City of London has overcome disasters such as the Great Fire of 1666 and the Blitz of World War II to become one of the world's leading financial centers. Bankers and traders flood into the city from the suburbs (though the stereotype of city gents in bowler hats is long gone), swelling the Square Mile's streets during the day, heading for modern skyscrapers such as Lord Foster's Gherkin. High-tech new buildings squeeze in alongside Sir Christopher Wren's architectural legacy of 17C churches, exemplified by the iconic dome of St Paul's Cathedral.

Centered around Westminster Abbey, the coronation venue of kings and queens for almost a millenia, Westminster is a hive of dynamic activity, while the grandeur of Buckingham Palace is just a short walk from the cosmopolitan nightlife of the West End. Hunt for bargains along the hustle and bustle of Oxford Street; enjoy an exotic meal in Chinatown; or while away the afternoon browsing the shop windows of luxury stores in opulent Mayfair. Alternatively, simply sit at a street café and relax while watching the street entertainers and musicians on the piazza of Covent Garden.

Located between Fulham to the west and Westminster to the east, Kensington and Chelsea are renowned for the exclusive addresses of Sloane Square and South Kensington. This is reflected in the serenity of their green parks, especially Hyde Park and Holland Park, and the chic stores and boutiques of Knightsbridge, the King's Road, and Notting Hill.

South Bank at dusk

www.southbanklondon.com

Cultural attractions such as the Royal Albert Hall, the Chelsea Flower Show, and the Notting Hill Carnival also highlight the distinctive characters of these twin royal boroughs.

The East End is the epitome of London's proud heritage and sense of community, where visitors can enjoy the traditional curry houses of Brick Lane, take a historical journey in the Tower of London, or discover the latest in Brit Art in the bohemian art galleries of Hoxton and Shoreditch. Regeneration projects such as the Olympic Park in Stratford exemplify the vigor and vim of the area, which was at the center of the world's attention during London 2012 and continues to benefit from its legacy.

Across the river from Westminster, the boroughs of Southwark, Lambeth, and Wandsworth are steeped in a rich literary history, from Shakespeare to Dickens. This cultural influence is embodied in the Southbank Centre, a hub of theaters and galleries. Industrial buildings now (or soon to be) put to new use, such as Tate Modern and Battersea Power Station, are architectural landmarks along this stretch of the River Thames.

Home to some of London's most desirable residences and leafy avenues, Camden and Islington personify the village feel of London's suburbs, while at the same time encompassing a rumpus of restaurants, theaters, and shopping precincts, all a short distance to the north of the City. Among the many sights to be seen are the street/alternative fashions of Camden Lock Market, the Tudor elegance of Charterhouse,

Tour bus at the Houses of Parliament

©John Samson, Presslink Communications/The Original Tour

and the picturesque squares of Bloomsbury.

It's well worth venturing away from the city center and into the lesser-known suburbs to escape the crowds and to discover some of the interesting districts that are a little off the normal tourist track. To the west lie Chiswick and Richmond, not to mention the royal palaces of Hampton Court and Windsor Castle. To the south lies Wimbledon, famed for its annual tennis tournament. To the north is Hampstead, with its affluent village, and to the east lie the pleasant vistas of Greenwich and the Docklands.

London also offers a variety of wonderful museums and galleries. The British Museum hosts a fascinating collection from every world civilization set around the stunning Great Court. Visitors can enjoy cultural institutions that showcase every important art movement from the Renaissance to Surrealism, decorative arts from Ming vases to the Rococo, and the extent of human endeavor that has helped shape our past and present.

CITY OF WESTMINSTER

The City of Westminster is home to the monarchy, the government, and many key tourist attractions. Like a pop-up book of iconic sights, a single bus ride or walk can take in the elegance of Trafalgar Square, the energetic color of Covent Garden and Soho, the grandeur of Westminster Abbey, or the pageantry of the Houses of Parliament.

WESTMINSTER

Houses of Parliament (Palace of Westminster)★★★

⊖*Westminster. 0844 847 1672. www.parliament.uk. Guided tours (75min). Call or see website for details.*

Westminster Palace, on the north bank of the Thames, is the meeting place of the two houses of the British Parliament—the House of Commons and the House of Lords. The first palace on the site, built by William I, served as the home of Parliament until 1512, when it was destroyed by fire. In 1547 the Commons were granted St Stephen's Chapel to use as their chamber, where they sat until the 19C. The Lords, nearly blown up in the **Gunpowder Plot** (1605), continued to meet in the White Hall until 1834 when a devastating fire swept through the palace. The new Parliament buildings, designed by Charles Barry and Augustus Pugin, were completed in 1860.

Don't miss:

- **Robing Room★** Where the sovereign dons the Imperial State Crown and crimson parliamentary robe.
- **Royal Gallery** (110ft/33.5m). Decorated with frescoes, statues, and portraits of all the sovereigns since George I. The **Prince's Chamber** displays paintings of Tudor monarchs.
- **House of Lords★★** At one end of the sumptuous chamber is the throne set under a Gothic canopy. The Woolsack, symbol of England's medieval power, is the seat of the lord chancellor.
- **Central Lobby★** The hub of the building, where many a well-known British political figure may be spotted.
- **House of Commons★** The chamber, destroyed in an air raid in 1941, was rebuilt without decoration. The green benches provide seating for 437 of the 651 elected members. In front of the Speaker's chair is the table bearing the mace and despatch

The Gunpowder Plot

In 1605 an attempt was made to blow up the House of Lords, the king and queen, and heir to the throne. A group of conspirators rented a cellar extending under Parliament and enlisted Guy Fawkes, a little-known mercenary from York, to plant explosives. The plot was discovered and under torture Fawkes revealed the names of his fellow conspirators. Two of the plotters were killed while resisting arrest; the others were tried, hanged, drawn, and quartered on January 31, 1606. Guy Fawkes Day is celebrated every November 5 with fireworks.

boxes. The **terrace** is reserved for Members and their guests.

- **St Stephen's Hall** This long, narrow hall was constructed to look like the original 14C St Stephen's Chapel.
- **Westminster Hall★** Built in 1097, the hall was used throughout the Middle Ages for royal feasts, jousts, and ceremonial occasions. Sir Thomas More (1535), Guy Fawkes (1606), and Charles I all stood trial here. Don't miss the superb **hammerbeam roof★★★**.
- **St Stephen's Crypt (St Mary's Chapel)** The domestic chapel built (1292–97) by Edward I.
- **Big Ben's Clock Tower★** St Stephen's clock tower (316ft/97m) was completed in 1859. The name **Big Ben** originally applied only to the bell, cast at the Whitechapel Foundry.
- **New and Old Palace Yards** contain the Jubilee Fountain and statues of Oliver Cromwell and Richard the Lionheart.
- **Victoria Tower★** This tower (336ft/102m) was built to house parliamentary documents. The statuary in the gardens includes a cast of Rodin's *The Burghers of Calais* and a statue of suffragette leader Emmeline Pankhurst.

- **Jewel Tower** *020 7222 2219. www.english-heritage.org.uk. Open daily 10am–5pm (Nov–Mar 4pm). £4.* This L-shaped tower dates from 1365 when it was built as the king's personal jewel house and treasury.

⋙ Walking Tour
See map pp 26–27.
✕**Lunch stop** – Cafés in and around Tothill Street.

▷ *Start from Westminster Bridge, then cross to Parliament Sq.*

Westminster Bridge★ – Has a fine view of the Houses of Parliament. At the foot of the bridge is a statue of Boadicea.

Parliament Square – Laid out in 1750 and redesigned in 1951, the square boasts statues of Victorian statesmen and a powerful statue of Churchill by Ivor Roberts-Jones.

▷ *Cross the square to the south and walk past St Margaret's Church and Westminster Abbey (see p 28).*

The old buildings of **The Sanctuary** serve as a marked contrast to the 1970s **Queen Elizabeth II Conference Centre** and **Central**

Houses of Parliament

©David Joyner/iStockphoto.com

CITY OF WESTMINSTER

25

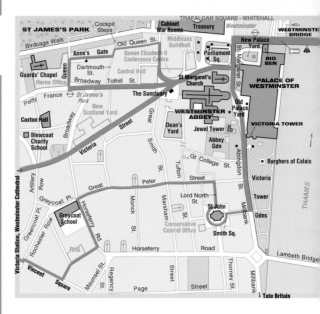

Hall opposite, designed as a Wesleyan church with the third-largest dome in London.

◗ *Walk up Storey's Gate and turn left into Old Queen St, lined with several 18C houses (note no. 28).*

Cockpit Steps now lead to Birdcage Walk and **St James's Park★★** (*see Parks and Gardens*) but in the days of Whitehall Palace they led down to a cockfighting pit. Flanked by the Home Office buildings on the left is **Queen Anne's Gate**, an L-shaped street of substantial early 18C houses.

◗ *Take Broadway and Tothill St to the top of Victoria St.*

Victoria Street is lined with 20C buildings, including: **New Scotland Yard** (1967); **London**

Transport's headquarters (1927–29); **Caxton Hall** (1878); the old **Blewcoat Charity School** (*Buckingham Street*) (1709). **Victoria Railway Station** was built in the 1870s, but the present buildings date from the 1900s.

◗ *Walk back to Westminster Cathedral Piazza, turn right into Ambrosden Ave, walk up Francis St, and make for the north side of Vincent Sq.*

Laid out in 1810 to provide playing fields for **Westminster School** (*see p 28*), **Vincent Square** is home to the buildings of the **Royal Horticultural Society** (f. 1804), which holds monthly flower shows (*open to nonmembers*).

St Margaret's Church★

⊖*Westminster. Open daily.*
The Parliamentary Church built by Edward I has undergone several phases of reconstruction over the years. St Margaret's is the parish church of the House of Commons mainly due to a tradition that began on Palm Sunday 1614 when the Commons met for the first time for corporate communion and, being mostly Puritans, preferred the church to the abbey. The interior has several Tudor monuments as well as memorials to Caxton, who is buried in the old churchyard, and Walter Raleigh, who was executed in Old Palace Yard in 1618 and buried beneath the high altar. The east window was made in 1501 at the request of Ferdinand and Isabella of Spain to celebrate the marriage of their daughter to Prince Arthur.

◗ *Walk along Elverton St and turn left into Horseferry Rd.*

Greycoat School (Greycoat Pl), a Westminster Charity school, was founded in 1698.

◗ *Walk along Great Peter St and turn right into Lord North St.*

With its many Georgian houses, today **Smith Square** is associated with politics; in the southwest corner is **Conservative Central Office** while many of the properties house MPs' offices or lodgings. At the center stands **St John's, Smith Square**, a tall Baroque church (1714–28), which now serves as a concert hall.

◗ *Take Dean Stanley St and turn left into Millbank to return to Parliament Sq.*

Westminster Cathedral★

⊖*Victoria. Cathedral Piazza, Victoria St. 020 7798 9055. www.westminstercathedral.org.uk. Open daily 8am–7pm (public holidays 5.30pm).*
The remarkable neo-Byzantine Roman Catholic cathedral is set back from Victoria Street and graced by a modern piazza. Construction began in 1895 and it was largely completed by 1903. The brick building is distinguished by a domed campanile (273ft/83m high). Inside the initial impression is of vastness and fine proportions. The nave, the widest in England, is roofed by three domes and the altar is dominated by a suspended crucifix. The decor, however, is incomplete, with the upper surfaces of the walls still awaiting mosaics.

CITY OF WESTMINSTER

Westminster Abbey

Westminster Abbey★★★

⊖*Westminster. 020 7222 5152.*
www.westminster-abbey.org. Open
daily 9.30am–3.30pm (Wed 6pm,
Sat 1.30pm), Sun for services only.
Pyx Chamber & Chapter House:
10am–4pm. Cloisters: 9am–6pm.
Museum: 10.30am–4pm. £18.
Westminster Abbey is as rich in
architectural splendor as it is in
history and culture. Since the
coronation of William I in 1066, all
but two of the kings and queens of
England have been crowned here.

What's inside?

- **Nave** The soaring vaulting
  retains all its original beauty. At
  the western end is the memorial
  to the **Unknown Warrior**. On
  the north side are tombs and
  memorials to famous musicians.
  Statemen's Aisle contains the
  graves and memorials of famous
  national figures.
- **Sanctuary** Where the monarch
  is crowned and receives the
  peers' homage in the coronation
  ceremony.
- The 13C **choir screen**.
- **Henry VII's Chapel★** contains
  the tomb of Henry VII. Beyond,

in the **RAF Chapel**, is the **Battle
of Britain Memorial Window**
(1947). In the south aisle are the
tombs of Mary Queen of Scots,
Charles II, William III and Mary,
and Queen Anne.

- **Queen Elizabeth Chapel**
  The white marble tomb of
  Elizabeth I lies above the
  unadorned coffin of Mary
  Tudor. At the east end is a small
  sarcophagus containing the
  bones thought to be those of
  the Little Princes found in the
  Tower of London.
- **Chapel of Edward the
  Confessor★★** contains the
  tombs of five kings and three
  queens around the Confessor's
  Shrine.
- **Poets' Corner★** This corner of
  the south transept contains the
  tomb of Chaucer and memorials
  to distinguished authors such
  as William Shakespeare, John
  Milton, and William Blake.

What's outside?

- **Great Cloisters** contain a
  number of historic buildings
  including the **Chapter House**,
  which served as the House of
  Commons under Edward I, and
  the **Chapel of the Pyx**, the
  monastery treasury during
  the 13C–14C.
- **Museum** Housed in the low
  vaulted Norman undercroft, it
  contains historical documents,
  gold plate, and unique wax and
  wood funeral effigies.
- **Dean's Yard** The old heart of the
  Abbey precinct; to the east a
  low arch leads to **Westminster
  School** (private). On the south
  side is **Church House** (1940),
  where the General Synod of the
  Church of England meets.

MUST SEE

ST JAMES'S★★

⊖*Piccadilly Circus; Green Park.*
St James's is one of London's most exclusive addresses. This elegant area is home to a royal palace and garden, dignified mansions, gentlemen's clubs, traditional pubs, specialist shops, and theaters.

St James's Street★ – This street was lined with town houses by the end of the 17C, including those of merchants who fled the City after the Plague and Great Fire (1665–66). It retains an air of quiet elegance with shops, restaurants, and clubs. Just off the street you'll find **Jermyn Street★**, crammed with shops selling luxury goods *(see Shopping),* and **Piccadilly Arcade★**, with its bow-fronted shops.

St James's Square★ – This large square, with its Classical equestrian statue of William III (1807), is encircled by modern offices and 19C residences except on the north and west sides where there are still Georgian town houses.

Carlton House Terrace★ – **Carlton House** (1709), George IV's fabulous mansion, was demolished in 1829, and John Nash, who had

Piccadilly Arcade
D. Chapuis/MICHELIN

just redeveloped Regent's Park, was commissioned to design a range of similar terraces here; only two were built. Between the two terraces at the top of steps leading down to the Mall, is the **Duke of York's Column**. In the nearby **Waterloo Place★**, designed by John Nash as an approach to Carlton House, stands the **Crimea Monument**.

St James's Church★
197 Piccadilly. 020 7734 4511. www.st-james-piccadilly.org. Open daily. Market: Tue 10am–6pm (antiques), Wed–Sat 11am–6pm (crafts).
Designed by Wren in 1676, this church boasts a fine Venetian window, an altarpiece of gilded wood carved by Grinling Gibbons, and a marble font in the form of the tree of life. The organ was donated by Queen Mary, daughter of James II. There are also lunchtime and evening recitals *(see Live Music).*

Spencer House
27 St James's Pl. 020 7499 8620. www.spencerhouse.co.uk. Guided tour (1hr) Sun (except Jan and Aug) 10.30am–5.45pm. £12. No children under 10yrs.
The house, built in 1756–66 for John, 1st Earl Spencer, is a pioneer of the Neoclassical style. After a decade of restoration it has now regained its late-18C splendor.

Green Park – *See Parks and Gardens.*
Queen's Chapel★ – *See Royal London.*
St James's Palace★★ – *See Royal London.*
Theatre Royal Haymarket★ – *See Stage and Screen.*

CITY OF WESTMINSTER

STRAND – TEMPLE★★

⊖ *Charing Cross.*

On the edge of the City, the Strand holds many attractions despite the relentless traffic. Fleet Street and Temple are intrinsic parts of entirely different traditions: the national press and British law.

•◦Walking Tour

✕ **Lunch stop** – Tom's Kitchen, Somerset House.

◗ *Start from Charing Cross Station.*

Strand★ – The elegant **Coutts Bank** building *(no. 440)* was designed by Sir Frederick Gibberd. Across the Strand, in Craven St, is **Benjamin Franklin House** *(no. 36; 020 7839 2006; www.benjamin franklinhouse.org)*, where the statesman lived between 1757 and 1775. In the forecourt of **Charing**

Cross Station is a reproduction of the **Eleanor Cross**, which once stood in Trafalgar Square.

◗ *Walk down Villiers St to* **Hungerford Bridge**, *then take Savoy Pl to Buckingham St.*

Buckingham Street *(River side)* 17C and 18C houses line its sides. Pepys lived at no. 12. At the south end is **York Water Gate**.

◗ *Continue to John Adam St and walk around.*

The riverfront retains the name **Adelphi** although the Royal Adelphi Terrace built by Adam in 1768–72 was demolished in 1937. George Bernard Shaw lived at no. 10a. No. 8 John Adam Street was built for the **Royal Society of Arts** in 1772–74 by Adam.

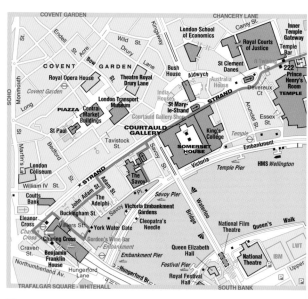

▶ *Return to the Strand via Adam St.*

🏛 **The Savoy** – The complex includes a **hotel**, one of the most famous in London, a **theater**, home of the D'Oyly Carte Opera Company who staged Gilbert and Sullivan's operettas, and a **chapel** (*Savoy Hill*), dating back to the 14C.

◯ *Walk down Savoy Hill to Victoria Embankment Gardens.*

Opposite **Victoria Embankment Gardens★** (*see Parks and Gardens*) stands **Cleopatra's Needle**, an Egyptian obelisk from c 1450 BC.

◯ *Walk back to the Strand and cross Lancaster Pl.*

🏛 **Somerset House★★** – Built in 1776–86, Somerset House now houses major art collections, including **The Courtauld**

Marcus Ginns/Somerset House

Somerset House

Gallery★★ (*see Great Galleries*). The grand piazza is used for public entertainment throughout the year, including concerts and an open-air cinema in summer and an ice rink in winter (*advance booking necessary*). Fine **views★★** of the Thames can be enjoyed from **Tom's Terrace** café (*May–Sept, 020 7845 4600. www.somersethouse.org.uk*).

The compact **St Mary-le-Strand** (1714–24) (*020 7538 5758; www.stmarylestrand.org*) is known as the "Cabbies church." Founded in 1829, **King's College** was housed from its earliest days in the east extension of Somerset House. The sweeping semicircle of the **Aldwych**, laid out in 1905, is occupied by massive buildings: Australia House, India House, and, in the center, **Bush House**, base of the BBC External Services.

St Clement Danes★ – *020 7242 2380. Open daily 9am–4pm.* Designed by Wren in 1682 on the site of a 9C church, the building was burned down on May 10, 1941 and rebuilt as the RAF church in 1955–58. A carillon rings out the **nursery rhyme** *"Oranges and lemons say the bells of St Clement's"* four times a day (*9am, noon (except Sun), 3pm (except Sun), and 6pm*).

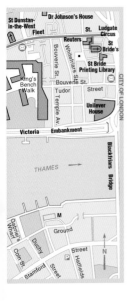

No. 216 the Strand is **Twinings**, a very old tea shop, and a little farther on, **Lloyd's Law Courts Bank Branch** *(no. 222)* is housed in the former Palsgrave Tavern, frequented by Ben Jonson. The famous **Wig and Pen Club**, which survived the Great Fire (1666), was at nos. 229/230. The **Royal Courts of Justice**, dating from 1874 to 1882, contain the vaulted Great Hall and early law courts.

At this point, the Strand gives way to Fleet Street within the confines of the City of London: the boundary is marked by the Temple Bar. Named after the River Fleet, **Fleet Street** was once synonymous with the press; the street has changed in character since the age of technology ousted all the national newspaper publishers.

▷ *Pass through **Inner Temple Gateway** (1610) to Temple.*

Temple★★ – Highlights include:

- **Temple Church**★★ *(020 7353 8559; www.templechurch.com)*, one of the most historic and beautiful churches in London, with over 800 years of history dating from the 12C Crusaders onward.
- **Middle Temple Hall**★★ *(020 7427 4800; www.middletemple.org.uk)* where, according to tradition, Elizabeth I watched the first performance of Shakespeare's *Twelfth Night* (1602).
- The **Master's House**, rebuilt in 17C style.
- The **Inner Temple Hall**, rebuilt after being damaged in the Blitz.
- **King's Bench Walk**, with a range of buildings by Wren.

Temple

The Knights Templars, who settled here after the Crusades, began building their church in 1185. In 1608 the church and the outlying property was granted to lawyers who formed themselves into three Societies: the Inner, Middle, and Outer Temples (the latter has long since disappeared). Today the area is abuzz with lawyers during the week and a haven of peace at weekends; at night, it is lit by gaslight.

▷ *Return to Fleet St and walk east.*

On the south side of Fleet Street stands **The Old Cock Tavern** and at no. 17 is **Prince Henry's Room**, its upstairs tavern room crammed with Samuel Pepys mementoes. **St Dunstan-in-the-West** *(020 7405 1929; www.stdunstaninthewest.org)* was built in 1833 by John Shaw.

▷ *Turn into Hind Court to Gough Sq.*

Dr Johnson's House★ *(17 Gough Sq; 020 7353 3745; www.drjohnsons house.org)*, was home to the great scholar and lexicographer between 1748 and 1759 and where he completed his *Dictionary* (pub. 1755).

▷ *Return to Fleet St, pass Shoe La, then cross to the south side.*

In among all the former newspaper buildings is **St Bride's**★ *(020 7427 0133; www.stbrides.com)*, boasting Wren's tallest white **spire**★★ (226ft/69m). The **St Bride Printing Library** and the **Punch Tavern** are located nearby.

➤ *End your walk at Ludgate Circus.*

PICCADILLY★

⊖Piccadilly Circus; Green Park; Hyde Park Corner.

This busy thoroughfare, lined with stately buildings, elegant shops, and luxury hotels, is the dividing line between fashionable Mayfair and dignified St James's. Don't miss the foody wonderland that is **Fortnum & Mason**, founded in 1707 *(see Afternoon Tea; Shopping).*

Piccadilly Circus★ – The circus, with its illuminated hoardings, is the beating heart of night-time London, located between the West End theaters and the clubs and restaurants of Soho. The statue of Eros, officially the Angel of Christian Charity, serves as a famous London meeting spot. The south side of the circus is occupied by the **Criterion**, a Victorian building containing a hotel and restaurant; the nearby **Criterion Theatre** was one of the first theaters to be lit by electricity.

Apsley House★

149 Piccadilly. 020 7499 5676. www.english-heritage.org.uk. Open Wed–Sun, public holidays 11am–5pm (Nov–Mar 4pm).

Home of the first Duke of Wellington, Apsley House stands on the site of the old lodge of Hyde Park. It was purchased by Wellington in 1817, having been designed nearly 40 years earlier by Robert Adam for Baron Apsley. The duke then transformed it to house his priceless collection of treasures. The **Wellington Museum**★ displays the duke's personal items, such as his uniforms, medals, and sword, as well as his collections of gold and silver plate, china, and snuffboxes. His outstanding art collection, housed in the **Waterloo Gallery**, includes many famous works.

Burlington House★

Piccadilly.

The former Earl of Burlington's town house is now home to the **Royal Academy of Arts** *(see Great Galleries)*. The gated **Burlington Arcade** (1819), a delectable (if expensive) retail experience, is patrolled by uniformed beadles.

Ritz Hotel

150 Piccadilly. 020 7300 2345. www.theritzlondon.com

This decorous and decadent hotel was opened on May 24, 1906 by César Ritz, a Swiss waiter turned entrepreneur. Regular patrons have included royalty (the Duke of Windsor and Wallis Simpson), the rich (Aristotle Onassis), and the famous (Charlie Chaplin, Winston Churchill). Tea at the Ritz is the height of the English experience – Earl Grey, cucumber sandwiches, and cream scones, with a harpist in the corner *(book well in advance).*

Academy of Arts – *See Great Galleries.*

Trocadero – *See For Kids.*

©English Heritage Photo Library

Waterloo Gallery, Apsley House

TRAFALGAR SQUARE – WHITEHALL★★

⊖ *Charing Cross; Westminster.*

Since its pedestrianization Trafalgar Square has lost most of the traffic but its famous column, lions, and fountains continue to be a congregation point in times of strife or great joy: political rallies, carols around the Christmas tree, or for the traditional New Year's Eve party.

⚞ Walking Tour

✕ **Lunch stop** – Café in the Crypt, St Martin-in-the-Fields.

Trafalgar Square★★ – The square, which celebrates Britain's naval prowess following Nelson's victory at the Battle of Trafalgar (October 21, 1805), was laid out by John Nash in 1820; the fountains were added in 1845 and remodeled in 1939 by Lutyens. The majestic piazza has steps sweeping down from the **National Gallery★★★** *(see Great Galleries)*, **Nelson's Column** rises from a pedestal, supported by Landseer's four magnificent bronze lions, and the long-empty fourth plinth – originally intended to hold an equestrian statue of William IV – has since 2005 held a series of temporary artworks, determined by public vote.

St Martin-in-the-Fields★ – *020 7766 1100. Open daily 8am–6pm. Lunchtime recitals: Mon–Tue & Fri 1pm. Evening concerts: Tue–Sat 7.30pm. Café in the Crypt & Market daily.* The church is known not only for its architecture and, since the 1930s, as a shelter for the homeless, but also for giving its name to the world-famous chamber orchestra the **Academy of St Martin-in-the-Fields** *(see Live Music)*. In the vaulted crypt is the **London Brass Rubbing Centre** *(see For Kids)*, while the courtyard hosts a lively arts and crafts **market**.

▷ *Walk up St Martin's La.*

Beyond the Post Office stands the striking Edwardian **Coliseum**, home to the English National Opera *(see Stage and Screen)*.

▷ *Retrace your steps to Whitehall and cross to the west side.*

The equestrian statue of **Charles I**, cast in Covent Garden in 1633, was set up in 1675 overlooking his execution site. From this point mileages from London are measured *(plaque in pavement behind statue)*.

Whitehall★★ – Named after the old Tudor palace that once stood here, this broad street is lined with government offices. The **Old Admiralty★** building was screened by a Classical portico by Adam in 1759–61. The adjacent

Trafalgar Square

J. Strachan/MICHELIN

Admiralty Arch, across the Mall, was constructed in 1906–11 by Sir Aston Webb.

Try not to miss the ceremonial mounting of the Queen's Life Guard at **Horse Guards★★★** – *See For Kids.*

◗ *Cross for **Banqueting House★★** (see Royal London).*

The 18C **Dover** and **Gwydyr Houses,** home to the **Scotland** and **Wales Offices**, face each other across Whitehall. In front of the monolithic **Ministry of Defence** building stands a small bronze of **Sir Walter Raleigh**, who was beheaded nearby. The façade of **Richmond Terrace**, dating from 1822, has been restored.

◗ *Cross the street again.*

Treasuries have stood on this site since the 16C; the present one dates from 1845.

Downing Street – No. 10 has been the residence of the prime minister since 1731 when Sir Robert Walpole accepted it from George II. The chancellor of the exchequer officially lives at No. 11.

The Cenotaph – The slim white monument by Lutyens (1919) is the country's official war memorial. A service is held here on Remembrance Sunday (the

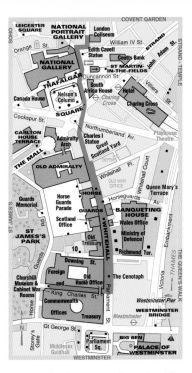

Sunday nearest to November 11) in the presence of the Queen.

◗ *Walk down King Charles St.*

Churchill War Rooms★★ – *King Charles St. 020 7930 6961. www.iwm.org.uk. Open daily 9.30am–6pm. Closed Dec 24–26. £17.50. Cafeteria.* The underground emergency accommodation built to protect Winston Churchill, his War Cabinet, and the chiefs of staff was the nerve center of the war effort from 1939 to 1945. There are 19 rooms on view, including the room from which Churchill made direct broadcasts to the nation. His private quarters house a **museum** focusing on the great statesman.

COVENT GARDEN★★

⊖ *Covent Garden.*

The refurbishment of the opera house and its facilities have given a new cachet to Covent Garden, which harks back to its heyday in the 19C. Old warehouses have been turned into enticing boutiques, while long-established businesses continue to thrive. Street cafés and entertainers cater to the browsers by day and smart restaurants feed the throngs of theatergoers by night. Don't miss the two traditional old-school clubs that still flourish nearby: the **Garrick** *(15 Garrick St)*, founded in 1831 and named after the actor, and the **Beefsteak** *(9 Irving St)*, a dining club dating from 1876. The picturesque **Neal's Yard★**, complete with old hoists, dovecote, and windowboxes has attracted a range of eco-friendly shops.

The Piazza★★ – Designed by Inigo Jones, London's first square followed the Italian model, lined on two sides with terraces of tall houses rising above a stone colonnade sheltering shops and coffee houses. Today the piazza is a meeting place for Londoners and visitors alike for relaxation and entertainment.

Bow Street – It was here in the mid-18C that the Bow Street Runners were established—the forerunner of the modern police force. The present building dates from 1881; in 1992 the police moved to new premises at Charing Cross.

Seven Dials – So-named because a 40ft/12m column, with a sundial on each face, was erected at the

Juggler Covent Garden Piazza

©Imagestate/Tips Images

center of seven radiating streets in the early 1690s. The column was pulled down by a mob in 1773 on a rumor that treasure was buried under it. A replica pillar has been erected on the original site.

St Paul's Church★

Entrance from Bedford St.

Since its completion in 1663, Inigo Jones's church has been associated with the world of entertainment. Overlooking the square, its portico provides a dramatic backdrop to a variety of street entertainers.

St Giles-in-the-Fields

60 St Giles High St. 020 7240 2532. www.stgilesonline.org.

This church, which is of ancient foundation, was rebuilt in 1734 in the Palladian style.

Covent Garden Market – *See Markets.*
London Transport Museum★ – *See For Kids.*
Royal Opera House★ – *See Live Music.*
Theatre Royal Drury Lane – *See Stage and Screen.*

MUST SEE

SOHO★

◯ *Leicester Sq; Piccadilly Circus; Tottenham Court Rd.*

Soho, the beating heart of the West End, is one of the greatest theater centers in the world. By day it is the hub of London's creative industries; by night it takes on new life as the clubs, bars, restaurants, cinemas, and theaters are thronged with night owls. Soho has its louche side, with risqué shows and shops, but it has a solid core of loyal residents among its otherwise transient population.

Chinatown★ – Gerrard Street, the center of this colorful area marked by oriental gates, abounds in restaurants, exotic supermarkets, and oriental medicine centers. It is the scene of great festivities at Chinese New Year celebrated in traditional fashion. **Old Compton Street**, at the heart of Soho, is lined with pubs, eating places, wine merchants, pastry shops, and Italian delis, and frequented by a spirited gay crowd. Nearby **Wardour Street** and its immediate vicinity conjure up the film industry from the creators of blockbuster movies and catchy commercials.

Leicester Square★ – The square, now a pedestrian precinct surrounded by cinemas and eating houses, is one of the busiest meeting places in London and the traditional site for red-carpet premieres. At its center stands the Shakespeare Memorial Fountain facing a statue of Charlie Chaplin. On the south side of the central garden is the **Half-Price Ticket Booth** (*see Stage and Screen*).

Soho Square – This pleasant square laid out in 1680 is adorned by a fountain topped by a statue of Charles II. Two churches stand to the east and northwest.

House of St Barnabas
1 Greek St. 020 7437 1894. www.hosb.org.uk. Check times before visiting.
The House of Charity, built c 1750, has one of the finest interiors in Soho, with beautiful plasterwork ceilings and walls, and a small French Gothic-style chapel (1863).

Regent Street★★ – *See Shopping.*
Carnaby Street – *See Shopping.*
Berwick Street Market – *See Markets.*

www.chinatownlondon.org

Chinatown

CITY OF WESTMINSTER

MARYLEBONE★

⊖ *Baker St; Regent's Park; Bond St.*
The appeal of Marylebone lies in
the contrast between the bustle of
Oxford Street★ and the calmness
of the dignified residential squares.
Famous department stores, elegant
outlets along **Wigmore Street**,
and tiny shops in quaint alleyways
make for a shopper's paradise. There
are also splendid 18C mansions
built for high society, one of which
is now home to the **Wallace
Collection★★★**. **Harley Street**
is famous as a center of medical
expertise, and cultural interest is
provided by **Broadcasting House**,
the home of the BBC, and
Wigmore Hall.

Oxford Street★ – London's main
shopping center, with major
department stores and high-street
shops. Just off Oxford Street is
St Christopher's Place, a narrow
pedestrian passage renowned for
its outdoor cafés and boutiques.
Around the corner in Regent Street
is **Hamleys**, one of the world's best
toy shops *(see Shopping)*.

Manchester Square – An
elegant square surrounded with
late Georgian houses, located to
the south of Manchester House,
which now houses the **Wallace
Collection★★★** *(see Major Museums)*.

Portland Place – A fashionable
promenade in the 18C, the street
is now home to the Art Deco
Broadcasting House (1931),
base of BBC Radio, and to **All Souls
Church** *(020 7580 3522; www.all
souls.org)*, designed by John
Nash. Its unique circular portico
of tall pillars is topped by a ring of
columns supporting a fluted spire.

Elementary,
My Dear Watson!

Baker Street was 100 years old
when Conan Doyle invented
221b as the address of his
famous detective Sherlock
Holmes; the highest number
was then 85 as the street was in
two sections. Hansom cabs, gas
lamps, and fog have gone, but
221b now exists as the street
was renumbered in 1930.

Sherlock Holmes Museum
*221b Baker St. 020 7935 8866.
www.sherlock-holmes.co.uk.
Open daily 9.30am–6pm. £10.*
The interior of this narrow
town house, built in 1815, has
been arranged as described in
the novels by Sir Arthur Conan
Doyle, including the familiar
pipes, deerstalker hat, and
magnifying glass.

St Marylebone Church
*Marylebone Rd. 020 7935 7315.
www.stmarylebone.org.*
The early 19C church where
Elizabeth Barrett and Robert
Browning were secretly
married in 1846.

St Peter's
*Vere St. 020 7399 9555.
www.licc.org.uk.*
This attractive, small, dark brick
building has an unexpectedly
spacious interior and beautiful
Burne-Jones stained-glass
windows.

MadameTussauds★ – *See ForKids.*
Wigmore Hall – *See Live Music.*

MAYFAIR★

⊖ *Bond St; Green Park.*

Mayfair is synonymous with elegance and luxury; **Bond Street★** runs through the middle, its shop-windows full of rare and exquisite goods. The luxury hotels along **Park Lane** overlook the green expanse of **Hyde Park★★** *(see Parks and Gardens)*. The area retains its prestige with numerous art galleries, auction houses, casinos, boutiques, and restaurants frequented by glamorous socialites.

Bond Street★ – Bisecting Mayfair from north to south is Bond Street. **New Bond Street** was built in 1720 and soon boasted such residents as Nelson, Byron, and Beau Brummell. Renowned for retailing elegance, the street is lined with designer and haute couture shops. At no. 35 is **Sotheby's** *(see Shopping)*, the biggest art auctioneer in the world—their first big sale on February 9, 1798 was of Marie Antoinette's pictures. Beyond the bronze group of Churchill and Roosevelt extends **Old Bond Street★**, lined with well-established shops selling fine porcelain and jewelry.

Shepherd Market★ – A maze of alleyways and paved courts linked by archways forms the market, which has Victorian and Edwardian pubs, pavement cafés, boutiques, and antique shops.

Grosvenor Square – The square (1725), one of London's largest, was redesigned in the 20C. Since 1961, it has been home to the American embassy (though this will move in 2017, to Wandsworth) and almost all of the surrounding buildings are US State Department offices. The central garden has a memorial to Franklin Roosevelt and a monument to the RAF American squadrons.

St George's Church
Hanover Sq. 020 7629 0874. www.stgeorgeshanoversquare.org. Open Mon–Fri 8am–4pm (Wed 6pm) and Sun 8am–noon.
The church (1721–24) is a distinctive landmark with its imposing Classical portico. Since it was first built, the church has been renowned for its society weddings, including those of Shelley, Disraeli, and Teddy Roosevelt.

Old Bond Street

Tony Latham / age fotostock

CITY OF WESTMINSTER

39

CITY OF LONDON

The City of London, also known as the Square Mile, is a compact area on the north bank of the Thames, associated with finance. Animated by a commuting workforce on weekdays, at night and weekends it tends to fall silent, its historic buildings and high-rise office blocks enjoyed only by a tiny population of Barbican residents and a few nightclub-goers.

THE CITY

St Paul's Cathedral ★★★

⊖ St Paul's. 020 7246 8357. www.stpauls.co.uk. Open Mon–Sat 8.30am–4pm (last admission), Sun for services only. Galleries: 9.30am–4.15pm. £16.50.

The imposing dome of St Paul's has dominated London's skyline for centuries and is one of the city's most enduring sights. Ever since the cathedral first rose out of the ashes of the Great Fire (1666), it has been a talisman for Londoners. Designed by Sir Christopher Wren, who is buried within its walls, the cathedral took 32 years to complete. St Paul's saw the funerals of Lord Nelson, the Duke of Wellington, and Sir Winston Churchill, and it was here on July 29, 1981 that HRH Prince Charles married Lady Diana Spencer.

St Paul's Cathedral

©Peter Smith/St Paul's Cathedral

The highlights

♦ **Interior** The marble high altar is set below a vast carved and gilded baldachin. The **organ** (late 17C) towers on either side of the opening to the choir, with its carved oak **choir stalls★★** by Grinling Gibbons. Among the many monuments and sculptures is a graceful Virgin and Child by Henry Moore (1984).

♦ **Dome★★** *Entrance in the south transept.* From the **Whispering Gallery★★** *(259 steps)* there is an impressive view of the cathedral far below, and a closer view of the dome frescoes by Thornhill. A hushed word uttered near the wall can be clearly heard by a person standing on the opposite side. The **Stone Gallery★** *(378 steps)* provides a good, but less extensive, **view★★★** of the City rooftops than the one from the **Golden Gallery** *(530 steps).*

♦ **Crypt** *Entrance in the south transept.* Grouped in bays are the tombs and memorials of men and women who have contributed to national life. **Artists' Corner** honors, among others, Christopher Wren, William Blake, JMW Turner, Sir Joshua Reynolds, and Holman Hunt. Down the steps is Wellington's sarcophagus and below the dome lies Nelson beneath a curving black marble sarcophagus.

- **The Treasury** displays plate and embroidered vestments.

Sir John Soane's Museum★★

13 Lincoln's Inn Fields. 020 7405 2107. www.soane.org. Open Tue–Sat 10am–5pm (last entry 4.30pm). No charge.

This museum offers an insight into the mind of a British collector of the early 19C. The varied exhibits, housed in small rooms and narrow passages, include casts and models, the sarcophagus of pharaoh Seti I (c 1392 BC), and architectural drawings. The **collection of pictures★★** includes works by Piranesi, Hogarth, Canaletto, Reynolds, and Turner.

Guildhall★

Gresham St. 020 7606 3030. www.guildhall.cityoflondon.gov. uk. Open (civic functions permitting) Mon–Sat 10am–4.30pm, Sun May–Sept only.

For at least 850 years Guildhall has been the seat of civic government. Work on the building began in 1411 and, the outer walls and crypt having survived the Great Fire and the Blitz, it is the only secular stone structure dating from before 1666 still standing in the City.

Don't miss:

- **Crypt** *Guided tours by appointment Mon–Fri.* The largest medieval crypts in London; the east crypt dates back to 1042.
- **The Old Library and Print Room** Designed by Sir Horace Jones and built in 1870.
- **Clock Museum★** *020 7332 1868. Open Mon–Sat 9.30am–4.45pm.* A display of 700 timepieces from the 15C to the 20C.

Sir John Soane's Museum

Martin Charles/Sir John Soane's Museum

- **Guildhall Art Gallery** *020 7332 3700 . www.guildhall-art-gallery. org.uk. Open Mon–Sat 10am–5pm, Sun noon–4pm.* The art collection owned by the Corporation of London includes portraits of dignitaries (17C–20C), 18C paintings, and works by the Pre-Raphaelites. A Roman amphitheater, unearthed in 1988, is now part of the Gallery.

London Bridge★

The only crossing over the lower Thames until 1750, London Bridge was once lined with houses, shops, and even a chapel; it was here that traitors' heads were displayed. In winter, when the river froze over, great Frost Fairs were held. In 1831 John Rennie constructed a robust granite bridge, 60yd/55m upstream, which was replaced in 1973 by the present sleek crossing; Rennie's bridge was sold for £1 million and removed to Arizona, USA.

Monument★

⊖ *Bank: Cornhill exit. 020 7626 2717, www.themonument.info. Open daily, Apr–Sep 9.30am–6pm, Oct–Mar 5.30pm. £4.*

41

The fluted Doric stone column, topped with a square viewing platform and gilded, flaming urn, was erected in 1671–77 to commemorate the Great Fire. The hollow shaft stands 202ft/62m tall and 202ft/62m from the baker's house in Pudding Lane where the fire began. The **view★** from the platform *(311 steps)* is now largely obscured by high-rise office blocks.

Mansion House★
⊖ *Bank: Cornhill exit. 020 7397 9306. Tours most Tues 2pm, call to confirm. £7.*
This Palladian-style mansion in Portland stone (1739–52) is the residence of the Lord Mayor. The interior is designed as a suite of magnificent state rooms with displays of **plate and insignia★★**, including the Lord Mayor's chain of office and the 18C Great Mace.

College of Arms
Queen Victoria St. 020 7248 2762. www.college-of-arms.gov.uk. Open Mon–Fri 10am–4pm.
The College dates from 1671 to 1688 and is responsible for granting coats of arms. It also undertakes genealogical research and organizes State ceremonies. The Earl Marshal's Court, the main room, is paneled and furnished with a throne and a gallery.

Goldsmiths' Hall
Foster La. 020 7606 7010. www.thegoldsmiths.co.uk. For details of Open Day tours, call City Information Office 020 7606 3030.
This grand hall dates from 1835 and boasts an exceptional collection of gold and silver plate. Its Baroque interior provides a lavish setting for its annual summer exhibition, plus a number of smaller exhibitions and fairs held throughout the year.

Smithfield London Central Markets
⊖ *Barbican; Farringdon. Charterhouse St.*
Smithfield opened as a meat, poultry, and provision market in 1868. Previously livestock had been driven into the City through Islington. The 8 acres/3ha of listed buildings boast 15 miles/24km of rails capable of hanging 60,000 sides of beef. Following its £70 million facelift, meat and provisions are still traded here (arrive early in the morning to see it in action).

Museum of London★★ –
See Major Museums.
Barbican Arts Centre –
See Live Music.

The Great Fire
The Monument was erected near the point where the Great Fire began in the king's baker's house in Pudding Lane; it ended at Pie Corner, near Smithfield. The flames, fanned by a strong east wind, raged for two days before slackening on the third. It was thought to be extinguished when it burst out again in the evening at the Temple; adjoining houses were demolished with gunpowder to prevent it spreading farther. People escaped with what they could carry by boat or on foot to Moorfields or the hills of Hampstead and Highgate.

THE CITY AND THE LAW

Central Criminal Court, the Old Bailey

Corner of Newgate St and Old Bailey. www.cityoflondon.gov. uk. Public galleries, Mon–Fri 10am–1pm and 2pm–5pm.

This is the third Criminal Court to occupy this site. The building is crowned by the **Lady of Justice**, a gold figure (12ft/3.5m tall) holding scales and a sword perched on a green copper dome (1907). Inside all is marble, a grand staircase sweeping up to halls decked with murals; the four original courts are paneled in carved oak.

Lincoln's Inn★★

020 7405 1393. www.lincolnsinn. org.uk. Precincts: Mon–Fri 7am–7pm. Chapel: Mon–Fri 9am–5pm. Old Hall, New Hall, and Library: Guided tour (min. 15 people) on written application only.

The mansion and grounds were bequeathed by the Earl of Lincoln (d. 1311) as a residential college, or inn, for young lawyers. The main gateway leads to several courts and beautiful gardens. The **Stone Buildings** date from 1775–80. The red-brick mid-19C **New Hall** and **Library** are diapered in the Tudor manner. The **Old Hall** dates from 1490. The **chapel** was rebuilt in 1619–23. The gabled brick buildings south of the court, known as the **Old Buildings**, are Tudor in style (redone in 1609). The **gatehouse** on Chancery Lane, with its corner towers and original oak doors, dates from 1518.

Gray's Inn★

020 7458 7800. www.graysinn.info. Gardens: Mon–Fri noon–2.30pm.

Gray's Inn, founded in the 14C and extended in the 16C, was largely rebuilt after the war. The main entrance is through the 1688 **Gatehouse**. **South Square** boasts a statue of Sir Francis Bacon, the Inn's most illustrious member. The **hall**, which was destroyed by fire, was rebuilt in its 16C style.

New Hall and Library, Lincoln's Inn

CITY OF LONDON

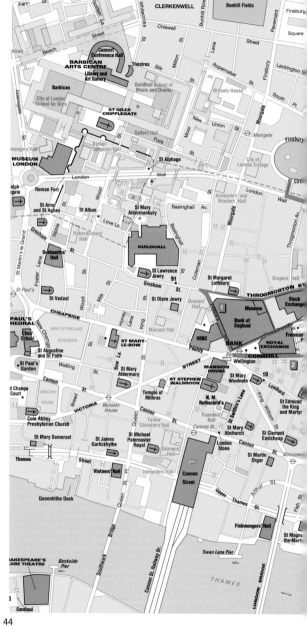

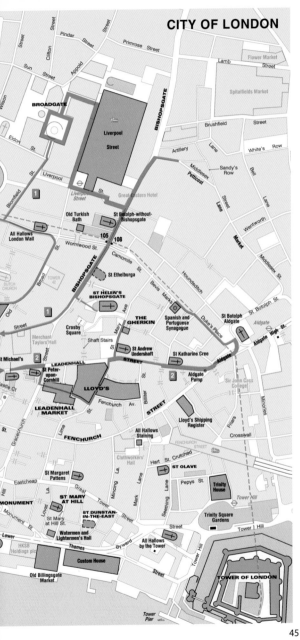

Street
Pindar Street
Clifton Street
Primrose Street
Sun Street
Wilson Street
Appold Street
Lamb Street
Flower Market
Spitalfields Market

BROADGATE

Liverpool Street

BISHOPSGATE

Brushfield Street
White's Row
Artillery Lane
Middlesex Street
Sandy's Row
Bell Lane
Petticoat Lane
Wentworth Street
Market
Middlesex St.

Eldon St.
Liverpool St.
Blomfield St.

Liverpool Street
Great Eastern Hotel

1

Old Turkish Bath
St Botolph-without-Bishopsgate

All Hallows London Wall
Wormwood St.
105 108
Camomile St.
Houndsditch

DUTCH CHURCH
Broad St.
TOWER 42
BISHOPSGATE
St Ethelburga
St Botolph St.
St Botolph Aldgate
Aldgate

ST HELEN'S BISHOPSGATE
Bevis Marks
Aldgate High St.

Old Street
1
Crosby Square
St Mary Axe
THE GHERKIN
Spanish and Portuguese Synagogue
Duke's Place

Merchant Taylors' Hall
Shaft Stairs

St Michael's
2
St Andrew Undershaft
St Katharine Cree
Aldgate
Aldgate Pump

LEADENHALL STREET
St Peter-upon-Cornhill
2
Sir John Cass College

Castle Ct.
Gracechurch St.
LLOYD'S
Fenchurch Av.
Billiter St.

LEADENHALL MARKET
FENCHURCH STREET
Lime St.
Lloyd's Shipping Register
Friars
Crosswall
Minories

All Hallows Staining
FENCHURCH STREET
Clothworkers' Hall
Hart St. Crutched Friars

St Margaret Pattens
Mincing La.
Mark Lane
ST OLAVE
Pepys St.
Trinity House

MONUMENT
Eastcheap
ST MARY AT HILL
Lovat La.
Great Tower Street
Seething Lane
Trinity Square Gardens
Tower Hill

Monument St.
St Mary at Hill St.
ST DUNSTAN-IN-THE-EAST
Byward Street
Tower Hill

Lower Thames St.
Watermen and Lightermen's Hall
All Hallows by the Tower
Tower Hill

HKSB Holdings plc
Custom House
Lower Thames Street
Tower Pier
TOWER OF LONDON

Old Billingsgate Market

45

CITY CHURCHES

There have been churches in the Square Mile since Saxon times. By 1666, there were 100, of which 87 were destroyed by the Great Fire and 51 rebuilt under the supervision of Wren. Nearly all suffered damage in World War II, but as the floor plans survived, it was possible for some to be reconstructed. Today there are 40 Anglican churches and five non-Anglican churches, making a total of 45 churches in the City. *For more information visit the City Information Centre (St Paul's Churchyard, EC4M 8AE; 020 7332 1456; www.visitthe city.co.uk).*

St Bartholomew-the-Great★★ – *West Smithfield. 020 7606 5171. www.greatstbarts.com. Open Mon–Fri 8.30am–5pm, Sat 10.30am–4pm, Sun 8.30am–8pm.* Only the chancel remains of the original great church of St Bartholomew's. Founded in 1123 as a priory, it was dissolved by Henry VIII in 1539, after which the church fell into disrepair and was not fully restored until 1910. Inside, the **choir★** is Norman. The 15C oak doors (by the

west door) lead to the old cloister (c 1405, rebuilt early 21C). The font, used at Hogarth's baptism in 1697, dates from the early 15C and is one of the oldest in the City.

St Stephen Walbrook★ – *Walbrook. 020 7626 9000. www. ststephenwalbrook.net. Open Mon–Fri 10am–4pm.* The most striking feature of this church is Wren's **dome★**, which undoubtedly served as a model for that of St Paul's, which it predates. Below the dome sits Henry Moore's monumental altar (1986).

St Mary-le-Bow★★ – *Cheapside. 020 7248 5139. www.stmarylebow. co.uk. Open Mon–Wed 7.30am–6pm (Thu 6.30pm, Fri 4pm)* The tower contains the famous Bow Bells and supports Wren's most famous **spire★★** (1671–80) with a weather vane, a winged dragon, poised at the top. Built in Portland stone in 1673, the church was the most expensive of Wren's churches. The twin pulpits are used for the famous dialogues where two public figures debate moral points. The crypt dates from 1087.

THE BEST OF THE REST:
St Mary-at-Hill★★ – *Entrance between 6 and 7 St Mary-at-Hill. 020 7626 4184 (office).*
St Giles Cripplegate★ – *Fore St. 020 7638 1997.*
St Mary Abchurch★ – *Abchurch La.*
St Anne and St Agnes – *Gresham St. 020 7606 4986.*
St Lawrence Jewry – *Gresham St. 020 7600 9478.*
St Magnus-the-Martyr – *Lower Thames St. 020 7626 4481.*
St Martin-within-Ludgate – *Ludgate Hill. 020 7248 6054.*

Ornate pulpit and cupola of St Stephen Walbrook

K. Brett/MICHELIN

MUST SEE

☙WALKING TOURS

If visiting the area for the first time, start at **St Paul's★★★** before popping into **St Mary-le-Bow★★**, walking down past the **Bank of England**, **Mansion House★**, and the **Royal Exchange★**, and on to **Leadenhall Market** and the **Lloyd's building★★**. This route will provide an impression of the City's principal institutions and broad range of architectural styles. On the next few pages are two suggested routes that will afford a glimpse of the City in more detail.

Tour 1: Bank – Bishopsgate

⊖**Bank: Cornhill exit.**
See map pp 44–45.
✕ **Lunch stop** – Cafés in Broadgate.

Bank of England – "The Old Lady of Threadneedle Street" is housed in a huge, undistinguished building with façade sculptures of Britannia served by six bearers and guardians of wealth. The **museum★** (020 7601 5545; www. bankofengland.co.uk) illustrates the history of banking using interactive displays and exhibits including a £1 million note, gold bars, and examples of forgeries.

▷ Follow Princes St and turn right into Lothbury.

St Margaret Lothbury★ – 020 7726 4878. www.stml.org.uk. The present building, designed by Wren, features a slender **spire★** and a magnificent interior with remarkable **woodwork★**.

Old Stock Exchange – 8 Throgmorton St. Trading in stocks and shares originated in this country in the 17C. In 2004, the Stock Exchange moved to a new home in Paternoster Square, beside St Paul's.

▷ Continue along Broad St past Tower 42 and turn left onto London Wall.

On your right is the church of **All Hallows London Wall** (020 7588 2638; www.allhallowsonthewall.org) and farther along at **Finsbury Circus** you'll find the only bowling green in the City.

▷ Continue along Blomfield St.

The redeveloped area of **Broadgate** features fountains, sculptures, and an open-air arena, which becomes an ice rink in winter (020 7505 4000; www.broadgate.co.uk). Walk past **Liverpool Street Station** (1875), which looks like a vast iron Gothic cathedral, and off Bishopsgate to the right is Middlesex Street, famous as **Petticoat Lane market** (see Markets). There are two churches of interest along Bishopsgate. **St Botolph-without-Bishopsgate** (020 7588 3388; www.botolph.org.uk) was rebuilt

St Ethelburga

This early 15C church, which stood on Bishopsgate until destroyed by a terrorist bomb in 1993, was the City's smallest church and one of the few medieval buildings to survive the Great Fire (1666) and World War II. The church has been rebuilt to its original plan as three walls and much of the timber and fittings survived.

in 1725–29 on a 13C site. In the churchyard, the **Old Turkish Bath** (1895), decorated with glazed tiling, is now a restaurant.

St Helen's Bishopsgate★ *(020 7283 2231; www.st-helens.org.uk)* is a late Gothic church incorporating a small 12C parish church and a 13C conventual church. Restoration following damage by a terrorist bomb has returned the church to pre-Reformation airiness and lightness. Inside, note the small **Night Staircase** (c 1500) for nuns attending night services and the superb **monuments★★** and brasses, including the black marble tomb of Sir Thomas Gresham (d. 1579).

▶ *Turn left onto Bishopsgate, then right into Threadneedle St past the ornate façades of banks and the Merchant Taylors' Guild.*

Royal Exchange★ – Declared the Royal Exchange by Queen Elizabeth I in 1571, this is the third building to stand on the site. The wide steps, portico, and pediment provide an impressive entrance to an edifice that was once the very hub of the City.

Lloyd's building

©PhotoDisc, Inc.

Tour 2: Cornhill – Aldgate

⊖*Bank: Cornhill exit or start from* ⊖*Aldgate and do the tour in reverse. See map pp 44–45.*
✕**Lunch stop** – S&M Café, Leadenhall Market.

Cornhill, named after a medieval corn market, is one of the two hills upon which London was first built.

St Michael's – *020 7248 3826. www.st-michaels.org.uk. Open Mon– Fri 8am–5.30pm.* The four-tiered tower (1718–24) was designed by Nicholas Hawksmoor. The church was extensively remodeled in the 19C, but Wren's vault (1670–77) has survived; don't miss the large 18C wooden pelican. Walk along the alleys south of St Michael's and discover former coffee houses: the **Jamaica Wine House**, dating from 1652, and the 600-year-old **George and Vulture**, twice destroyed by fire.
St Peter-upon-Cornhill *(entrance from St Peter's Alley; 020 7283 2231)* claims to stand on the highest ground and on the oldest church site in the City. The present building (1677–87) was designed by Wren. Inside, the **oak screen★**, one of only two to survive in Wren's churches, the organ gallery, pulpit, and font are all original.

Leadenhall Market – *Gracechurch St.* A bustling food market at its best at the start of the shooting season and at Christmas *(see Markets).*

Lloyd's★★ – *020 7327 1000. www.lloyds.com. Opens once a year as part of London's Open House day; www.londonopenhouse.org.*

The trading activities of Lloyd's, the biggest insurance corporation in the world, are conducted in a striking steel and glass building (1986) designed by Sir Richard Rogers. The company dates back to 1691 when Edward Lloyd took over Pontaq's, a French-owned eating house, which became a meeting place for merchants, shippers, and bankers. Lloyd inaugurated the still current system of posting notices and lists of port agents, transport vessels, cargo shipment agents, and other such shipping intelligence.

▷ *Make a short detour to St Mary Axe.*

The Swiss Re Building – The 40-story Swiss Re Building (2004), better known as "the Gherkin," was designed by the UK's architectural superstars, Sir Norman Foster and Partners. Circular, bulging in the middle, and tapering as it soars into the sky, it is Britain's first environmentally sustainable high-rise.

St Andrew Undershaft – *020 7283 2231. Open by appointment.* This 16C church is named after the maypole that stood in front of it until 1517. The interior boasts some fine early **monuments★**, a late 16C–17C window, a Renatus Harris organ, and altar rails by Tijou (1704).

▷ *Continue along Leadenhall St.*

St Katharine Cree – *020 7283 5733. Open Mon–Fri 10.30am–4pm.* The present light and airy church, thought to be the third on the site, survived the Great Fire of 1666.

The Lutine Bell at Lloyd's

The **Lutine Bell** was retrieved from *HMS Lutine*, a captured French frigate that was sunk off the Netherlands in 1799 with gold and coins valued at nearly £1.5 million and insured by Lloyd's. Its bullion was partly salvaged in 1857–61. The bell is struck to mark the end of a crisis involving an overdue vessel: once for a loss, twice for a safe arrival.

Note the early 17C alabaster font, 18C pulpit, and altar table.

Aldgate – The original Roman gate, over which Chaucer lived in the 14C and through which Mary Tudor rode after being proclaimed queen, was demolished in 1761. The **Aldgate Pump** still stands at the west end of the street.

St Botolph Aldgate – *020 7283 1670. www.stbotolphs.org.uk.* There had been a church on this site for over 1,000 years when George Dance the Elder came to rebuild it (1741–44). Dance's interior was remodeled in the 19C: note in particular the plasterwork frieze decorating the coved ceiling.

▷ *Walk up Duke's Pl to Bevis Marks.*

Spanish and Portuguese Synagogue – *020 7626 1274, www.bevismarks.org. Open Sun–Fri 10.30am–2pm, Sun 12.30pm, Tue and Fri 1pm.* The oldest synagogue in England (1701) and the only one in the City. The building is functional except for the seven splendid brass chandeliers, lit for festive occasions.

KENSINGTON AND CHELSEA

Genteel and moneyed, Kensington and Chelsea is one of London's most elegant areas, knitted around a patchwork of squares, dazzling white town houses, and mews houses down leafy backstreets, with millionaire pricetags. The area cradles key London attractions, from South Kensington's museums to the shopping hubs of Kensington High Street, the King's Road, and trendy Notting Hill, with its bohemian village vibe, café culture, and the Portobello Road antiques market every Saturday.

CHELSEA★★

Chelsea is synonymous with a fashionable, if privileged, lifestyle. Its lively atmosphere, with a remaining air of 60s Bohemia, draws a trendy social scene. Explore the King's Road and the residential squares, and walk along Chelsea Embankment for views of the Thames, to appreciate the charm of the area.

There are plenty of elegant boutiques, antique shops, cafés, and restaurants to indulge one's fancy. For shoppers **Sloane Square**, boasting the stunning Peter Jones department store and the **Royal Court Theatre** (see Stage and Screen), is a must, while the **King's Road**, which was once the private route used by Charles II to visit Nell Gwynne in Fulham, is now famous for its shops, restaurants, and pubs (see Shopping).

The Royal Hospital★★

Royal Hospital Rd. 020 7881 5298.
www.chelsea-pensioners.org.uk.
Open Mon–Fri 10am–noon, 2–4pm.
No charge.

Chelsea Pensioners have been colorful members of the local community for over 300 years. In 1682 Charles II commissioned Sir Christopher Wren to build a veteran's hostel. The magnificent building has a main court open on the south to the grounds and the river. From the Octagon Porch steps rise on either side to the **Chapel and Great Hall**. The **Council Chamber** (west wing) was decorated by both Wren and Robert Adam; Van Dyck painted the portrait of Charles I and his family. The **Museum** displays Wellington mementoes and illustrates the history of the hospital. Since 1913 the Royal Horticultural Society's

Chelsea Pensioner, Royal Hospital

Tim Graham / age fotostock

MUST SEE

world-famous **Chelsea Flower Show** has been held in the grounds.

Cheyne Walk★
⊖*Sloane Sq.*

The terraces of fine brick houses along the river front are rich with memories of artists, writers, and royalty. At no. 4 George Eliot spent her last weeks. **Queen's House** *(no. 16)* was the home of Pre-Raphaelite poet and painter Dante Gabriel Rossetti. Nos. 19–26 occupy the site of Henry VIII's riverside palace. The artist Whistler lived at no. 96, while Turner (1775–1851) spent his last years at no. 119. **Lindsey House** (1674) on the site of Sir Thomas More's farm, was home to the Brunels. **Chelsea Old Church** *(020 7795 1019; www.chelseaoldchurch. org.uk)*, with a 14C chapel remodeled by Sir Thomas More in 1528, was reconstructed after bomb damage. **Chelsea Harbour**, where barges once unloaded coal, is now a riverside development centered around a 75-berth marina.

Carlyle's House
24 Cheyne Row. 020 7352 7087. www.nationaltrust.org.uk. Open Wed–Sun 11am–4.30pm.
Scottish historian Thomas Carlyle (1795–1881) lived in this modest Queen Anne brick house with his wife Jane Welsh. The four-storied house contains a wealth of memorabilia that reflect the couple's unpretentious lifestyle.

Holy Trinity
Sloane St. 020 7730 7270. www.holytrinitysloanesquare. co.uk. Open Mon–Fri 9am–6pm, Sat 9.30am–6pm. Concerts.
Rebuilt in 1888 by a leading exponent of the Arts and Crafts

Chelsea Luminaries

A varied group of notables have lived in Chelsea: actresses Nell Gwynne, Dame Ellen Terry, Dame Sybil Thorndyke; engineer Isambard Kingdom Brunel; novelist Elizabeth Gaskell; Pre-Raphaelites Dante Gabriel and Christina Rossetti, Burne-Jones, William Morris, Holman Hunt, Swinburne, and Millais. Other artists include William de Morgan and Augustus John. Mark Twain, Henry James, and TS Eliot are among Chelsea Americans. Oscar Wilde lived at 34 Tite Street; AA Milne at 13 Mallord Street.

movement, John Dando Sedding, the 48-panel east window is by Burne-Jones: the St Bartholomew panel is by William Morris.

St Luke's
Sydney St. 020 7351 7365. www.chelseaparish.org. To view, contact the Parish Office.
This Bath stone church (1820) is an early example of Gothic Revival and resembles King's College Chapel in Cambridge.

Chelsea Physic Garden – *See Parks and Gardens.*
National Army Museum★ – *See Major Museums.*
Saatchi Gallery – *See Great Galleries.*

KENSINGTON★★
The Royal Borough of Kensington takes pride in its aristocratic connections. Famous for its world-class **museums** and fashionable amenities, the green expanses of **Hyde Park and Kensington**

51

Gardens★★, and **Holland Park** *(see Parks and Gardens)* offer year-round attractions, while **Kensington Palace**★★ *(see Royal London)* gives the area its royal flavor. To the north lies Notting Hill, which boasts many excellent restaurants and bars.

Portobello Road★ comes to life on Saturdays with one of London's finest markets *(see Markets* and also hosts part of **Notting Hill Carnival** in August, Europe's largest street carnival *(see Calendar of Events)*.

Kensington High Street

Stylish and functional, Kensington High Street boasts all the usual chain stores, and can be less crowded than the West End.

The **Roof Garden** at no. 99 *(entrance in Derry St; 020 7937 7994; www.roofgardens.com.)*, was laid out in the 1930s and has mature trees, grass, and even flamingos. The **Commonwealth Institute** is dedicated to celebrating the different cultures of the 50 Commonwealth countries.

Walking Tour –

South Kensington

⊖ *Gloucester Rd.*
✕**Lunch stop** – Carluccio's, Old Brompton Rd.

The **Royal College of Art** (1961), has nurtured many famous artists, architects, and designers. The elaborately decorated building next to it is the former home of the **Royal College of Organists** (1875).

Royal Albert Hall★ – The hall, a red brick Victorian building almost

¼ mile (0.4km) in circumference, hosts the summer series of Promenade Concerts *(see Live Music)*. Virtually next door, the **Royal Geographical Society** founded in 1830, has been a cornerstone of Britain's exploration of the world ever since. The collections contain objects linked to the great explorers and the **Map Room** contains 30,000 historic maps *(020 7591 3000; www.rgs.org; Map Room and Library: Open Mon–Fri 10am–5pm)*.

To the south, in Prince Consort Road, is the **Royal College of Music**, built in 1893 in neo-Gothic style. Its highly prized **Museum of Instruments** has over 600 items, including a spinet played by Handel, and Haydn's clavichord *(020 7589 3643; www.rcm.ac.uk)*. The buildings of the **Imperial College of Science and Technology** extend south to the Science Museum.

Hyde Park Chapel *(Exhibition Rd)*, a Mormon chapel with a spire of gilded bricks, dates from 1960.

▷ *Continue past the Science*★★★, *Natural History*★★, *and V&A Museums* ★★★ *(see Major Museums); cross Cromwell Rd.*

Michelin House in Art Nouveau style

K. Brett/MICHELIN

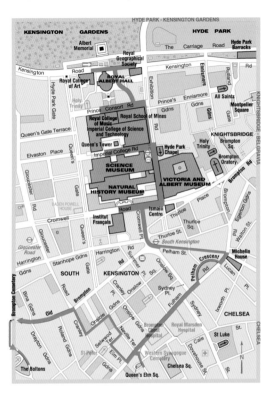

The distinctive **Ismaili Centre** serves as a religious and cultural center. Farther along, the Art Nouveau-style buildings of the **Institut Français** date from 1938.

○ *Retrace your steps and turn right into Cromwell Pl; turn left into Pelham St.*

Michelin House – The former UK headquarters of Michelin Tyre PLC, the original Art Nouveau **decoration★** has been restored and the tiled tire-fitting bays preserved.

○ *Walk along Fulham Rd past Pelham Cres and two hospitals.*

In **Queen's Elm Square** Elizabeth I is said to have sheltered under an elm during a storm. There are 19C artisan cottages in **Elm Place** *(across Fulham Rd and on the right).* Turn right past the pub, then left to **Onslow Gardens**, a mid-19C development of stuccoed houses.

○ *Cranley Gdns leads to Old Brompton Rd; turn left into Boltons Pl.*

The Boltons is a fine crescent of white-stuccoed houses. Farther on along Brompton Road is **Brompton Cemetery**, a vast 19C necropolis with neo-Gothic-, Egyptian- and Baroque-style tombs.

53

KNIGHTSBRIDGE – BELGRAVIA★★

Knightsbridge and Belgravia are the most exclusive residential districts in the capital, and the fashionable emporia and designer stores along Brompton Road, Sloane Street, and Beauchamp Place are temples of delight. The area also boasts some of the finest hotels and restaurants.

⚭ Walking Tour

✕**Lunch stop** – Harrods: Oyster bar; rotisserie; seafood grill.

◗ Start from Hyde Park Corner. (For **Apsley House★** see p 33.)

Lanesborough Hotel – This handsome building (1827–29) on Hyde Park Corner was originally designed by William Wilkins to house St George's Hospital.

◗ Walk down Knightsbridge; turn left into Wilton Pl.

The 17C brick terraces of **Wilton Place** predate St Paul's Church by a century, erected in 1843 on the site of a Guards barracks. **Wilton Crescent** is lined by stuccoed terraces.

◗ Make a short detour to Wilton Row to visit the Grenadier pub, then return to Belgrave Sq.

Belgrave Square★★ – The square (10 acres/4ha), home to several embassies, is bordered by twinned ranges of white-stuccoed houses with urns and balustrades, pillared porches, and decorative ironwork. A bronze statue of Simon Bolivar stands at the south-east corner. Seaford House was the residence of the statesman, Lord John Russell. **St Peter's Church**, at the north-eastern end of Eaton Square, was erected in 1827 in the Classical style, as part of the original development project. The interior was refurbished after a fire in 1988.

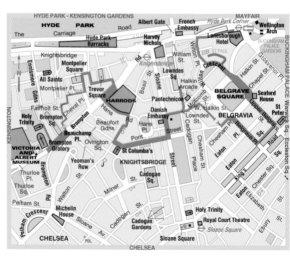

Lanesborough Hotel

©The Lanesborough, a St Regis Hotel

▷ *Proceed along Eaton Sq and Belgrave Pl, then turn left into Chesham Pl, through Belgrave Mews to Halkin Pl and West Halkin St.*

Pantechnicon – This Doric-columned warehouse dates from 1830. On either side and in West Halkin Street and Halkin Arcade are a number of small shops selling a range of luxury goods.
Just to the north is **Lowndes Square**, developed in the mid-19C and largely rebuilt in the 20C.

▷ *Walk back and turn right into Cadogan Pl toward Sloane St.*

Sloane Street – First developed in 1773 to link Knightsbridge to Chelsea and the river, the street has been rebuilt piecemeal. The Danish Embassy (1976–77) was designed by Ove Arup. The area west of Sloane Street, known as Hans Town, dates from the late 18C.

▷ *Turn right into Pont St.*

On the right is Hans Place, a pleasant residential area. On the left is **St Columba's**, the London Church of Scotland (1950–55) *(020 7584 2321; www.stcolumbas. org.uk).*

▷ *Turn right on Walton St; turn left on Hans Rd.*

Harrods – Founded in 1849, this shop is regularly voted one of the world's finest department stores *(see Shopping).*

▷ *Cross Brompton Rd and explore the charming streets and squares, past the following:*

Brompton Road – The triangle between Kensington Road and Brompton Road developed as a residential district around a series of squares: **Trevor Square** (1818), **Montpelier Square★** (1837), **Brompton Square** (1826). Narrow streets link the squares, with mews and closes lined with color-washed cottages.

Oratory of St Philip Neri (Brompton Oratory) – *020 7808 0900. www.bromptonoratory.com. Open daily 6am–8pm.* The main body of the church (1881) was built in the Italian Baroque style. The dome and lantern were designed so as to span the exceptionally wide and lofty nave.
Hidden behind Brompton Parish Church is the attractive garden of the early 19C **Holy Trinity Church**.

SOUTH BANK TO SOUTHWARK

Stretching along the south bank of the River Thames, opposite the City and Westminster, the South Bank and Southwark bustle with vibrancy and creative innovation. The perfect day out for culture vultures— whether enjoying a play at the South Bank Centre or installations at Tate Modern, leafing through secondhand bookstalls during a riverside walk, or shopping for gastronomic treats at Borough Market.

SOUTH BANK★★★

⊖ Waterloo.

Amble along the riverside for classic views of Westminster and live music, then stop for a drink in one of the many restaurants or bars. Next, browse the secondhand bookstalls under Waterloo Bridge, take in a show at the **National Theatre**, enjoy a concert at the **Royal Festival Hall★**, settle down to some classic movies at the **British Film Theatre**, or enjoy an exhibition at the **Hayward**—the choice is yours! The new image of the South Bank as a tourist hot spot is borne out by the crowds of visitors thronging to the attractions built to mark the third millennium, including the ever popular **London Eye★** *(see For Kids)*.

View from Waterloo Bridge

Y. Kanazawa/MICHELIN

County Hall★

Belvedere Rd.

Built in 1908, County Hall, a colonnaded arc some 700ft/213m in diameter, is still one of London's most distinctive buildings. Until 1986 it was the headquarters of the Greater London Council. It now houses two hotels, apartments, restaurants, and the **London Aquarium★** *(see For Kids)*, as well as an amusement arcade with the latest electronic games.

Southbank Centre★

After the war, bomb-damage debris was cleared from the riverside to make way for the 1951 Festival of Britain and a future arts center. The riverfront is now a lively area for tourists and locals, filled with walkways, shops, bars, restaurants, and cafés. Refurbishment of the 1960s arts center is underway.
Royal Festival Hall★ – A concert venue that now ranks among the greatest in the world *(see Live Music)*. In 1962–65 the river frontage was redesigned to include the main entrance and faced with Portland stone. There are refreshment facilities, and book and music shops in the foyer.
Queen Elizabeth Hall and Purcell Room – Two smaller concert venues *(see Live Music)*.
BFI IMAX – *0870 787 2525. www. bfi.org.uk.* Run by the British Film Institute, a state-of-the-art, large-

format cinema with surround-sound *(see Stage and Screen)*.
BFI Southbank (formerly known as the National Film Theatre) – One of the world's leading cinémathèques *(see Stage and Screen)*. The **Jubilee Gardens**, on the site of the 1951 Festival, were opened in 1977 to celebrate the 25th anniversary of the Queen's accession. The whole area has recently been redeveloped into a first-class park *(www.jubilee gardens.org.uk)*.

🚶 Riverside Walk

Apart from the attractions afforded by the arts complex and the London Eye, a riverside walk offers some stunning views across the river as well as some interesting sights along the way:

♦ **The South Bank Lion** gazes speculatively from a plinth at the foot of Westminster Bridge. Painted red, it was the mascot of the Lion Brewery until placed at the bridgefoot in 1952.

♦ In front of the **National Theatre** stands a statue of Sir Laurence Olivier as Hamlet, unveiled in September 2007.

♦ The sleek, five-arched concrete structure of **Waterloo Bridge** was designed by GG Scott in

National Theatre

Stephen Cummiskey/National Theatre

1945; it replaced the original bridge built by Rennie that was opened on the second anniversary of the Battle of Waterloo (June 18, 1815).

♦ **Gabriel's Wharf**, a lively workplace for craftspeople, has evolved alongside the gardens and low-cost housing of the Coin Street development *(020 7401 2255; www.coinstreet.org; open Tue–Sun 11am–6pm, bars and restaurants later)*.

♦ **Bernie Spain Gardens** is a pleasant sunken green space from which to enjoy the ever-changing spectacle on the river and the north bank.

♦ **Stamford Wharf** is marked by the **OXO Tower**, a former beef-extract factory now housing restaurants and designer studios.

♦ The **Bargehouse** houses temporary offbeat exhibitions.

Royal National Theatre★★ – *See Stage and Screen.*
London Eye★ – *See For Kids.*
Hayward Gallery – *See Great Galleries.*

4D Experience at the London Eye

A new attraction opened in 2009 at the London Eye: the 4D Experience. Wearing 3D glasses, visitors watch a four-minute-long 3D film while experiencing a fourth dimension created by in-theatre effects including wind, snow, rain, mist, and bubbles.

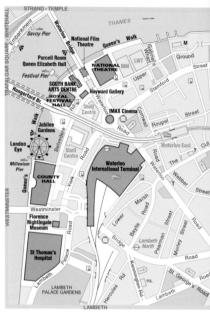

BANKSIDE★ TO SOUTHWARK★

The **Globe★★** and **Tate Modern★** are two potent symbols that combine history and modernity on Bankside, while the bustling **London Bridge** area (home to the recently completed **Shard★★**) and **Hay's Galleria** highlight the vitality of Southwark, which extends south from the Thames to Crystal Palace. After years of neglect, the area is becoming one of the trendiest in London, full of theaters, museums, bars, and restaurants—and a relaxed atmosphere that allows visitors to stroll and enjoy views of the river and the City skyline.

Tour 1: Along the River
◯ Southwark; Blackfriars (on the other side of the bridge).
✕**Lunch stop** – Hay's Galleria.

◯ From Blackfriars Bridge take Queen's Walk.

Bankside Gallery – 020 7928 7521. www.banksidegallery.com. Open daily 11am–6pm. The gallery, which opened in 1980, holds regular exhibitions under the aegis of the Royal Societies of Painters in Water Colours and of Painter-Etchers and Engravers.

Tate Modern★ – See Great Galleries.

Millennium Bridge – This pedestrian suspension bridge, designed by Sir Anthony Caro and Foster & Partners, forms "a blaze of light" spanning the Thames at night. After initial problems that nicknamed it "the wobbly bridge," it now provides a link between St

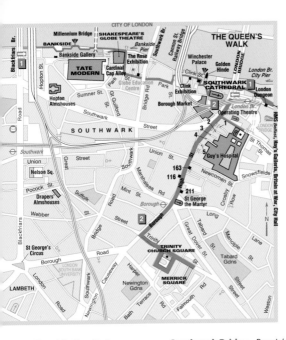

Paul's and the Tate Modern. Turn right into **Cardinal Cap Alley**. On either side are two 18C houses. The first, **no. 49**, is the oldest house on Bankside.

Shakespeare's Globe★★ – See Stage and Screen.

◗ Turn right into New Globe Walk and left into Park St.

The Rose Theatre Exhibition – 56 Park St. 020 7261 9565. www.rosetheatre.org.uk. Sat 10am-5pm. No charge. A light and sound show brings to life the history of the Rose Theatre, the first theater on Bankside (1587). The Rose Revealed Project is currently working on creating a new visitor centre here.

Southwark Bridge – Rennie's bridge (1815–19) was replaced in 1919 with the iron structure by Ernest George.

◗ Cross the road to view the ground plan of the original Globe Theatre. Continue to the end of the street and turn left to the riverfront.

Clink Exhibition – 1 Clink St. 020 7403 0900. www.clink.co.uk. Open daily 10am-9pm (Oct–Jun 6pm, weekends 7.30pm). £7.50. In a basement on the site of the old Clink jail, the exhibition traces the history of imprisonment and torture, and of Bankside's brothels.

Winchester Palace – The ruins of the Bishop of Winchester's Palace date from the 12C. In the 15C, the prison for errant clergy and

59

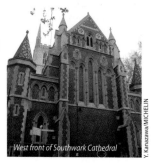

West front of Southwark Cathedral

Y. Kanazawa/MICHELIN

A 1C Roman road, vestiges of the Norman church, the medieval priory, and 17C–18C kilns can be viewed from the glazed link.

▷ Pass under **London Bridge**★ (see City of London).

View from the Shard★★ – Joiner St. 0844 499 7111. www.theviewfromtheshard.com. Open daily 10am–10pm. £24.95 in advance, £29.95 on the day. Completed in 2012 and designed by Renzo Piano, the Shard is London's latest landmark and the tallest building in the European Union. Take in the view (up to 40 miles on a clear day) from the 68th, 69th and 72nd floors – unarguably the best in London – or visit one of the 31st floor restaurants (See Restaurants).

London Dungeon – See For Kids.

Hay's Galleria – The original Hay's Dock has been sealed over and now boasts a 90ft/27m-high glass barrel vaulted roof. The converted warehouses now house shops, bars, and restaurants.

nuns housed in the palace's cellar became known as **Clink Prison**, from which the expression "to be in the clink" is derived.

St Mary Overie Dock – The full-scale replica of Sir Francis Drake's **Golden Hinde** is made of African iroko hardwood and caulked with oakum in the traditional way. The galleon is open for tours (See For Kids).

Southwark Cathedral★★ – 020 7367 6700. www.southwark. anglican.org. Open daily 8am (Sat, Sun 9.30am)–6pm. Donation £4. The Cathedral of St Saviour and St Mary Overie developed from an Augustinian priory (1106) to parish Church of St Saviour (1540) and, finally, to Cathedral (1905). The interior has some fine monuments and a sumptuous Gothic altar screen (1520). The **Harvard Chapel** is dedicated to John Harvard, the founder of Harvard University, USA, who was baptized in the church in 1607. The **Visitor Centre** (access from the north aisle or from the north door into Lancelot's Link) displays artifacts uncovered during excavations.

▷ The tour can continue along the riverside (Queen's Walk).

HMS Belfast – See For Kids.

Opposite the Tower of London, on a site where excavations have identified the precincts of Edward II's 14C Rosary Palace, sits London's **City Hall**, home of the Mayor's office and Greater London Assembly. Designed by Sir Norman Foster and partners, in the shape of a glass dish around a central spiral corridor, every aspect of the building was created to be environmentally friendly *(open to the public Mon–Thu 8.30am–6pm, Fri 8.30am–5.30pm).*

Tour 2: Borough

⊖ *London Bridge. See map pp 58–59.*
✕ **Lunch stop** – George Inn.

Borough High Street –
A vibrant area, full of historic street and inn names, it currently looks a bit neglected as buildings are being demolished to make way for the London Quarter Development. Don't miss **Borough Market** *(see Markets)* and the 17C **George Inn★**.

▷ *Turn left into St Thomas St.*

Old Operating Theatre, Museum, and Herb Garret –
9A St Thomas St. 020 7188 2679. www.thegarret.org.uk. Open daily 10.30am–5pm. £6.50.
The attic of St Thomas's Parish Church was already a herb garret when, in 1821, it was converted into a operating room for St Thomas' Hospital. Predating the advent of anesthetics, the amphitheater is ringed by five rows of "standings" for students.

Guy's Hospital – An imposing
complex that still retains its 18C railings, gateway, and forecourt.

▷ *Return to the High St.*

The Yards and the Inns of Southwark – Several narrow
streets and yards off the High Street mark the entrances to the old inns, the overnight stops of people arriving too late at night to cross the bridge into the capital.

King's Head Yard [1]: now a 19C building, sports a colored effigy of Henry VIII. **White Hart Yard** [2]: the pub (demolished) was the headquarters of Jack Cade in 1450. **George Inn★** [3]: part 17C galleried inn with tables in the cobbled yard in summer and open fires in winter. **Talbot Yard** [4]: mentioned by Chaucer in the Prologue of his *Canterbury Tales*. **Queen's Head Yard** [5]: site of the Queen's Head (demolished) sold by John Harvard before he set out for America. The **King's Arms** (1890) *(Newcomen St)* takes its name from the arms of George II that originally decorated the south gatehouse of old London Bridge.

St George the Martyr –
020 7357 7331. www.stgeorge-themartyr.co.uk.
The pulpit of this 1736 church is the highest in London.

▷ *Continue to the next crossroads and turn left into Trinity St.*

Trinity Church Square★ –
The statue in the central garden, known as King Alfred, is believed to be the oldest in London. The church (1824) was converted into a studio for major orchestras in 1975.

Merrick Square★ – An early
19C square with elegant lamp standards and modest houses.

SOUTH BANK TO SOUTHWARK

TOWER HILL AND EAST LONDON

The East End, an integral part of London, prides itself on its Cockney tradition, a tradition enriched by wave after wave of immigrants over the centuries. The vibrant multicultural scene is in sharp contrast to the historic splendor of Tower Hill and Greenwich, which lie to the west, and the modernistic Docklands development to the south. Since London won the bid for the 2012 Olympic Games the area has become a sea of redevelopment, bringing vital regeneration to the area.

GREENWICH★★★

⊖*North Greenwich; Rail: Greenwich from Charing Cross; Waterloo; London Bridge; Cannon St; DLR: Cutty Sark; by boat from Westminster or Tower Bridge.*

The glories of Greenwich are many: a wonderful riverside setting, a vast park, an attractive town with **historic inns**, antiques shops, and **market** *(see Markets)*, and world-famous **museums**. The riverside walk affords superb views of the **royal buildings** and modernistic skyline across the river. Straddle the **Greenwich Meridian**, from where all world time is set. The regenerated Greenwich Peninsula boasts the **Millennium Dome**, now the **02 Arena** concert venue and exhibition space.

Old Royal Naval College★★

020 8269 4747. www.ornc.org. Painted Hall & Chapel and Visitor Centre: Open daily 10am–5pm. Grounds: Open daily 8am–6pm.

The college's **Painted Hall★**, Wren's domed refectory, was completed in 1703. In 1805 Nelson lay in state here before his burial in St Paul's. The hall and upper hall were painted in exuberant Baroque style by Sir James Thornhill. Wren's **chapel★** was redecorated after a fire in 1779 in Wedgwood pastel colours. From **Cutty Sark Gardens**, the **Foot Tunnel** *(elevator or 100 steps; open 24 hrs)* leads under the Thames to the Isle of Dogs, from where there is a fine **view★★★** of Greenwich.

Old Royal Naval College and Queen's House and in the distance, the Royal Observatory

MUST SEE

Royal Observatory Greenwich★★

*020 8858 4422. www.rmg.co.uk.
Open daily 10am–5pm (last
admission 4.30pm). Closed
Dec 24–26. No charge.*

Built for Charles II in 1675 by
Sir Christopher Wren, the small
red brick observatory is named
after John Flamsteed, the first
Astronomer Royal. The **tour** begins
in the courtyard where visitors can
straddle the Greenwich Meridian,
the line of zero longitude linking
the north and south poles. The
red time ball on the roof of
Flamsteed House was erected
in 1833 to serve as a time check
for navigation on the Thames;
the ball rises to the top of the
mast and drops at exactly 1300
hours GMT. Inside, displays trace
the Observatory's history and the
evolution of astronomy.

The mid-18C **Meridian
Building** was built to house the
observatory's **collection**★★ of
instruments, including Britain's
largest refracting telescope.
Adjacent are the **Peter Harrison
Planetarium** and Weller
Astronomy Galleries, opened
in 2007.

Fan Museum★

*Crooms Hill. 020 8305 1441.
www.thefanmuseum.org.uk.
Open Tue–Sat 11am–5pm,
Sun noon–5pm.*

This delightful museum owns
3,500 fans from the 11C to the
present day, with strong
reference to the 18C and 19C.

Ranger's House★

*Chesterfield Walk, West Parkside.
020 8853 0035. www.english-
heritage.org.uk. Open Apr–Sept
Sun–Wed 11am–3.30pm, entry by
tour only, at 11am and 2pm. £6.90.*

This 18C villa provides a superb
setting for the **Wernher Collection**,
the eclectic taste of Sir Julius
Wernher (1850–1912), a mining
magnate and philanthropist.
The collection includes rare early
religious paintings, works by
Dutch Masters, jewelry, silverware,
ceramics, porcelain, and tapestries.

Cutty Sark★★ – *See For Kids.*
Greenwich Park – *See Parks
and Gardens.*
**National Maritime
Museum**★★★ – *See Major Museums.*
Queen's House★★ – *See Royal
London.*

Pawel Libera/Visit Britain

DOCKLANDS★

DLR or ⊖ Canary Wharf; by boat from Westminster or Tower Bridge.
The area opposite Greenwich has undergone a radical change since **Canary Wharf** was built in the 1980s. Set in a series of great loops in the Thames, this shimmering landmark overlooks a host of award-winning architecture.

Wapping – *⊖Tower Hill; DLR: Tower Gateway.*

Wapping was just a village until the 16C when the riverside sprawl began to develop. Dickens set several of his novels among the narrow alleys, steps, stages, and docks here.
Built at the beginning of the 19C, **St Katharine Dock★** takes its name from the **Hospital of St Katharine by the Tower**, founded in 1148 as a shelter for refugees. In 1968 the 19C dock basins were converted into a luxury yacht marina. The beautiful brick vaults and cast-iron structure of **Tobacco Dock★**, converted into a chic shopping mall, now lies largely empty while decisions are made about its future. Two historic ships are moored on the canal at the rear.

St Katharine Dock

Visit Britain

Limehouse – *DLR: Limehouse.*

Named after its lime kilns, this was a shipbuilding center. Its exotic street names and oriental restaurants are a reminder of the Chinese immigrants who settled here in the 18C.
Regent's Canal Dock (1820) once accommodated barges coming down to the Thames via the 1mi/1.6km long Limehouse Cut.

Isle of Dogs★ – *DLR: Between West India Quay and Island Gardens.*

Located in a huge loop in the Thames and cut off at the top by docks, the "island" has been transformed into a high-tech commercial alternative to the City. Development began early in the 19C when the **West India Docks** (1802–6) were built to receive rum and sugar from the West Indies. At the west end of the old import dock are the **Cannon Workshops,** now occupied by small businesses. To the north is the old **Dockmaster's House**. Dominated by the tallest tower block in London, **1 Canada Square** (800ft/244m), **Canary Wharf★★** also houses a concert hall, restaurants, pubs, open spaces, and two shopping malls.
Mudchute Park features a riding stable and small urban farm (*open daily 9.30am–4.30pm*).
The riverside **Island Gardens** (1895) provide a stunning **view★★★** of Greenwich and access to the **Greenwich Foot Tunnel** *(see p 62).*

Museum in Docklands★ –

West India Quay. 020 7001 9844. www.museumoflondon.org.uk/ docklands. Daily 10am–6pm. This award-winning museum covers every aspect of port activity with an interactive area for kids, costumed re-enactments, and guided walks along the Thames.

TOWER HILL AND BERMONDSEY★★

⊖*Tower Hill.*

Dominated by the historic **Tower of London**★★★ *(see Royal London)*, **Tower Hill** has preserved its traditional role as a place of free speech and a rallying point for protest marches, usually to Westminster.

🐾Walking Tour

✕**Lunch stop** – Butler's Wharf.

◗ *Start at Tower Hill Station.*

Trinity Square Gardens – The gardens include the site of the **scaffold and gallows** erected in 1455; the last execution was held in 1747.

◗ *Walk up Cooper's Row and turn left into Pepys St.*

St Olave's★ – *020 7488 4318. Open Mon–Fri 10am–5pm (except Aug).* This 15C church, restored in 1953, retains some impressive monuments. The churchyard gateway, decorated with skulls, is dated 1658.

◗ *Take Hart St west, walk down Mark La to Tower St and cross the busy main road.*

All Hallows-by-the-Tower – *020 7481 2928. www.allhallowsbythetower.org.uk. Open Mon–Fri 8am–5pm, Sat–Sun 10am–5pm.* The church boasts an exquisite wooden **font cover**★★ (Grinling Gibbons) and 18 exceptional **brasses**★ (1389–1591).

Tower Bridge
Pawel Libera/VisitLondon

◗ *Walk down Tower Hill and cross Tower Bridge to Bermondsey.*

Tower Bridge★★ – *020 7403 3761. www.towerbridge.org.uk. Open daily Apr–Sept 10am–6pm; Oct–Mar 9.30am–5.30pm (last entry 30min earlier).* The Gothic towers of Tower Bridge, built between 1886 and 1894, are linked by high-level footbridges that provide panoramic **views**★★★ and host the **Tower Bridge Exhibition** with displays on "Great Bridges of the World" and "The Sixties" *(see For Kids).*

Bermondsey – Located on the south bank of the Thames, the area has undergone extensive redevelopment and the riverfront around the old **Butler's Wharf** is alive with people enjoying the restaurants, bars, and wonderful river views. *For details of the Friday* **Bermondsey Market**, *see Markets.*

Design Museum – *Shad Thames. 020 7403 6933. www.designmuseum.org. Open daily 10am–5.45pm, last admission 5.15pm.* The museum opened in 1989 to popularize, explain, analyze, and criticize past and present design, and speculate about design in the future. The

Review Gallery on the first floor displays a selection of state-of-the-art products from around the world.

THE EAST END

Shoreditch
🚇 *Old St.*

The first English playhouse, **The Theatre**, was founded in Shoreditch in 1576 by James Burbage (d. 1597). In 1597 it was pulled down and the materials used by James' son Cuthbert to build the **Globe★** *(see Stage and Screen)*.

Hoxton Square – This working-class district gained a certain notoriety as artists and musicians moved in and set up their studios. Consequently there are now a number of bars, restaurants, and art galleries, which attract a Bohemian, trendy crowd.

St Leonard's Church – *119 Shoreditch High St. 020 7739 2063. Open by appt only.* This mid-18C church boasts a 192ft/58.5m spire. Within its precincts were buried one of Henry VIII's court jesters, William Somers (d. 1560), James Burbage (d. 1597) and his sons, and Gabriel Spencer (d. 1598), a player at the Rose Theatre who was killed by Ben Jonson.

Whitechapel Gallery

Guy Montagu-Pollock/Whitechapel Gallery

Spitalfields
🚇 *Shoreditch; Liverpool St.*

The eastern part of the Victorian structure is all that remains of **Old Spitalfields Market★**. In 1991 London's largest wholesale fruit and vegetable market moved to Leyton. Today, the vibrant and popular market sells fashion, jewelry, antiques, and organic produce *(see Markets)*. Across the street is **Christ Church**, built by Hawksmoor in 1714–30 *(020 7859 3035; www.christchurchspitalfields. org).* The church holds a number of events during the year, including the **Spitalfields Festival** *(020 7377 6793; www.spitalfieldsvenue.org).* Right next to Spitalfields is **Petticoat Lane Market** *(see Markets)*.

Brick Lane – The area known as "little Bangladesh," or "Bangla Town," can be crowded at weekends, but it is still a great place to go for a curry. The fact that the **mosque** was built as a Christian chapel in 1743 and later became a synagogue, reflects the successive waves of immigrants who have lived here. The glass-fronted reception of **Truman's Brewery** (1666) reveals older buildings around a cobbled yard. On Sunday mornings, a bric-a-brac and secondhand clothes **market** is held in the district *(see Markets)*.

Whitechapel
🚇 *Aldgate East.*

The **Whitechapel Bell Foundry** has been on its present site in Whitechapel Road since 1738. It has cast and recast—owing to the 1666 Great Fire and World War II—the bells of St Mary-le-Bow, St Clement Dane's, and Big Ben.

MUST SEE

Whitechapel Gallery – 020 7522 7888. www.whitechapelgallery.org. *Open Tue–Sun 11am–6pm (Thu 9pm).* The gallery displays modern and contemporary art by nonestablished artists; Barbara Hepworth and David Hockney first showed their work here. The building (1901) is decorated with contemporary Arts and Crafts reliefs.

Bethnal Green
⊖ *Shoreditch; Bethnal Green.*
St Matthew parish church was built (1743–46) by George Dance the Elder and the interior remodeled in 1859–61. The west tower of **Sir John Soane's St John's Church** (1825–28) is a real landmark as it rises to an attractive vaned cupola *(www.stjohnon bethnalgreen.org).*

Museum of Childhood at Bethnal Green – *See For Kids.*

West Ham
⊖ *Bromley By Bow.*

Three Mills – *Three Mill La. 020 8980 4626. www.housemill.org.uk.* At the end of the 19C there were about 300 companies in West Ham engaged in various industries. This attractive group of early industrial buildings includes **House Mill** (1776), the largest tide mill known in the country, the **miller's house**, reconstructed as part of a restored Georgian street front, and **Clock Mill**, which dates from 1817. **Abbey Mills Pumping Station**, that houses sewage pumping machinery, dates from 1865 to 1868.

Other East End Musts:
- **Geffrye Museum★** ⊖*Hoxton. Kingsland Rd. 020 7739 9893. www.geffrye-museum.org.uk. Open Tue–Sun 10am–5pm.* Housed in alms-houses erected in 1712–19, the museum features displays of furniture and furnishings from Tudor times to the 1950s.
- **Sutton House** ⊖*Bethnal Green. 2, 4 Homerton High St. 020 8986 2264. www.nationaltrust.org.uk.* This fine brick Tudor house, dating from c 1535, retains many original features, including oak paneling, a painted staircase, and Tudor transom windows.
- **William Morris Gallery** ⊖*Walthamstow Central. Lloyd Park, Forest Rd. 020 8527 3782. www.wmgallery.org.uk.* The museum, housed in a former home of the Morris family, concentrates on the work of William Morris (1834–96) and the firm Morris & Co. (1861–1940), which he co-founded.

BLOOMSBURY, CAMDEN, AND ISLINGTON

Liberal and elegant, Camden and Islington have historically had a cultured, creative vibe that is still evident today. Bloomsbury, with its literary connections, is a patchwork of genteel garden squares and home to the British Museum. Further north, Clerkenwell is full of urban style and warehouse conversions, whose residents socialize in Upper Street's bars and traditional pubs. Camden Town is a stroll from both Regent's Park and busy markets full of alternative style.

BLOOMSBURY★

⊖ *Tottenham Court Rd; Goodge St; Russell Sq; Holborn.*
The area, comprising many 18C and 19C squares, is dominated by London University and the **British Museum★★★**. Bloomsbury also contains a concentration of medical institutions, including The Hospital for Sick Children (Great Ormond Street), endowed by JM Barry with the royalties of *Peter Pan*.

⌇⌁Walking Tour

✕**Lunch stop** – Charlotte Street.

Bedford Square★★ – This elegant square was developed to designs by Thomas Leverton.

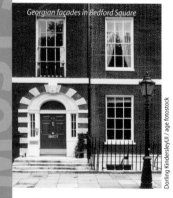
Georgian façades in Bedford Square

Dorling Kindersley UI / age fotostock

▷ *Proceed along Adeline Pl to Great Russell St.*

British Museum★★★ –
See Major Museums.

▷ *Turn right into Museum St.*

The Cartoon Museum –
35 Little Russell St. 020 7580 8155. www.cartoonmuseum.org. Open Mon–Sat 10.30am–5.30pm, Sun noon–5.30pm. The Cartoon Art Trust and its museum collect and exhibit humorous and satirical art works, drawings, engravings, illustrations, advertisements, comic strips, and animated films from the time of William Hogarth to the present.

▷ *Turn left into Bloomsbury Way.*

St George's Bloomsbury –
020 7242 1979. www.stgeorges bloomsbury.org.uk. Mon–Fri noon– 5.30pm. Hawksmoor's church (1716–31) has a pedimented portico and a steeple topped with a statue of King George I.

▷ *Continue to Bloomsbury Sq and turn left.*

Bloomsbury Square – One of the two mid-18C houses in the southwest corner was the former

MUST SEE

residence of Isaac and Benjamin Disraeli (1818–26).

◑ *Walk down Bedford Pl and through Russell Sq; proceed to Tavistock St. Right on Gower St.*

University College – The college houses the **Flaxman Sculpture Galleries** and a number of excellent **museums** *(www.ucl.ac.uk/museums)* attached to departments such as geology, zoology, and archeology. The **Petrie Collection** consists of 80,000 Egyptian and Sudanese artifacts housed in galleries so dark you need a torch. This is the northern end of **Museum Mile**, which runs to Somerset House.

◑ *Take Grafton Way to* **Fitzroy Square★** *(Virginia Woolf lived at no. 29). Left into Conway St; left on Maple St; right on Cleveland Mews.*

BT Tower – This landmark tower was erected in 1965 to provide an unimpeded path for London's telecommunications system.

Don't miss:

◆ **The Dickens House Museum**
⊖ *Russell Sq. 48 Doughty St. 020 7405 2127. www.dickens museum.com. Open Mon–Sun 10am–5pm (last admission 4pm). £8.* The only surviving London home of Charles Dickens, who lived here from 1837 to 1839. Original paintings, furniture, and authentic decor recreate his life, and the museum also holds readings, walks, and tours.

◆ **The Foundling Museum**
⊖ *Russell Sq. 40 Brunswick Sq. 020 7841 3600. www.foundling museum.org.uk. Open Tue–Sat 10am–5pm, Sun 11pm–5pm.* London's first home for abandoned children was a wholly philanthropic affair, founded by Thomas Coram and backed by luminaries such as Hogarth and Handel. Reopened as a museum, its impressive art collection includes British works by Hogarth, Gainsborough, and Reynolds.

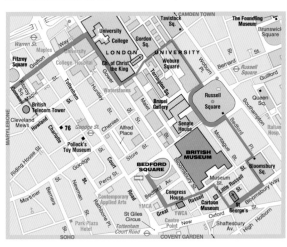

Camden Lock

C. Eyemenier/Michelin

♦ **Pollock's Toy Museum
and Shop** – *See For Kids.*

CAMDEN TOWN
⊖*Camden Town.*
Camden Town, with its delightful
village atmosphere, has pockets
of elegant houses sought after by
creative types. The ever-popular
markets, clubs, restaurants, and
Irish pubs lend it a Bohemian
atmosphere, especially at weekends.
From **Camden Lock** you can take
a boat up to the **Zoo** and **Little
Venice** or down to **Limehouse**.

Jewish Museum
*129–131 Albert St. 020 7284 7384.
www.jewishmuseum.org.uk.
Open Sun–Thu 10am–5pm, Fri
10am–2pm (last admission 30min
earlier). £7.50.*
The museum houses a large range
of exhibits including a medieval
mikveh, unearthed in London in
2002. You can wander down a 19C
East End street, and explore how
and why Jews have come here from
around the world and become part
of British life. The Holocaust is seen
through the eyes of a London-born
Auschwitz survivor *(not advised for
young children).*

Roundhouse
Chalk Farm Rd.
The 1840s former locomotive
shed, a listed building, has been
converted to provide television,
radio, and recording studios as well
as large and small theater
and music venue spaces, a glass-
covered restaurant, and garden.

Camden Lock Market –
See Markets.
Stables Antique Market –
See Markets.

ST PANCRAS
⊖*King's Cross-St Pancras.*
One of London's biggest rail
hubs, St Pancras lies on the edge
of Bloomsbury. The area is also
home to the British Library and its
improving tourist infrastructure
includes several quality hotels,
an improving restaurant scene,
and some interesting small
museums.

British Library★★
*96 Euston Rd. 0870 444 1500.
www.bl.uk. Open Mon–Sat
9.30am–8pm (Fri 6pm, Sat 5pm),
Sun 11am–5pm. No charge.*
While the new red-brick premises
have earned few compliments,
the **John Ritblat Gallery** presents
the library's great treasures,
including rare manuscripts,
Books of Hours, examples of
early printing, famous works
(Lindisfarne Gospel, Gutenberg
Bible), early maps, musical scores,
and historic documents such as
the Magna Carta, Essex's death
warrant, Nelson's last letter, and
Shakespeare's first folio (1623).
The Reading Rooms *(pass required)*
are quiet havens.

London Canal Museum

12–13 New Wharf Rd. 020 7713 0836. www.canalmuseum.org.uk.
The museum, housed in an old ice house on the Regent's Canal, explores the history of British canals.

CLERKENWELL

⊖*Barbican; Farringdon; Old St.*
The secluded character of Clerkenwell underwent a radical change in the 1990s when old warehouses were transformed and the trendsetters moved in, quickly followed by a range of select eateries and a popular clubbing scene.

Charterhouse★

Charterhouse Sq, 020 7253 9503, www.thecharterhouse.org. Guided tours Tue–Thu and Sat: 020 7251 5002 (book in advance). £10.
At every stage of its history—14C priory, Tudor mansion, 17C hospital and boys' school, 20C residence for aged Brothers—the Charterhouse buildings have been replaced or altered in a variety of styles. The Tudor **Great Hall** remains intact, as does **St John's Gate**, sole survivor of the Hospitallers buildings dismantled in 1546. The 20C Tudor-style **Chapter Hall** serves as a **museum** *(020 7324 4005; www.sja. org.uk/museum).* **St John's Church** once extended west into the square; the crypt is 12C, the only original priory building to survive.

Wesley's House and Chapel

49 City Rd. 020 7253 2262. www.wesleyschapel.org.uk.
Founded by the charismatic Methodist minister John Wesley in 1777. the chapel interior is notable for its Robert Adam ceiling and Wesley's mahogany pulpit. A **Museum of Methodism** is housed in the crypt.

Sadler's Wells Theatre – *See Live Music.*

ISLINGTON

⊖*Angel; Highbury and Islington.*
Islington's elegant Georgian squares, Victorian terraces, and proximity to the City ensure its popularity as a residential area. A curious mix of gentrification and dilapidation is reflected in its smart restaurants, bustling bars, antique shops, art cinema, and avant-garde theaters, which do a roaring trade alongside its street market.

Estorick Collection of Modern Italian Art

39a Canonbury Sq. 020 7704 9522. www.estorickcollection.com. Wed–Sat 11am–6pm, Sun noon–5pm. £5.
Housed in a grade-II listed Georgian building, the Estorick Collection is known internationally for its core of Italian Futurist works, as well as figurative art and sculpture dating from 1890 to the 1950s.

Camden Passage – *See Shopping.*

Tudor Great Hall, Charterhouse

K. Brett/MICHELIN

ROYAL LONDON

From the earliest times British sovereigns have built their palaces in and around London. From the Tower of London, one of the first royal residences which houses the glittering Crown Jewels, to Buckingham Palace, the official London residence of Britain's monarchs since 1837, these historic and fascinating buildings are not to be missed.

HAMPTON COURT★★★

Rail: Hampton Court from Waterloo. 0844 482 7777. www.hrp.org.uk. House: Open daily Mar–Oct 10am–6pm (last admission 5pm); Oct–Mar 10am–4.30pm. Formal gardens: 10am–6pm (winter 5.30pm) House & gardens £18.20 (£17.05 online), gardens only £5.72. See map p 100.

One of Henry VIII's favorite palaces, Hampton Court was the perfect rural retreat for many sovereigns, with its romantic setting by the Thames. The Tudor buildings are magnificent, enlarged and rebuilt by Henry VIII. The palace was extended in the late 17C with two ranges of handsome state apartments designed by Sir Christopher Wren for William and Mary. In summer, Hampton Court hosts the Flower Show, open-air concerts, and theater, while in the winter there's an open-air ice rink and Christmas evenings.

Hampton Court Palace

C. Ochterbeck/Michelin

What's inside?

♦ **Tudor Royal Lodgings**
   Entrance in Anne Boleyn's Gateway.
   Boasting the magnificent **Great Hall**, the **Chapel Royal**, and the **Haunted Gallery**, said to be visited by the ghost of Henry VII's fifth wife Catherine Howard.

♦ **Queen's State Apartments**
   Entrance in Clock Court. Lavishly decorated for Queen Anne.

♦ **King's Apartments** *Entrance in Clock Court.*

♦ **Georgian Rooms** *Entrance in Fountain Court.*

♦ **Wolsey Rooms and Renaissance Picture Gallery**
   Entrance in Clock Court.

♦ **Tudor Kitchens** *Entrance in Clock Court.* The largest and most complete kitchens to survive from the period.

What's outside?

♦ The **Trophy Gates,** built in the reign of George II.

♦ The **moat and bridge,** constructed by Henry VIII.

♦ The **Great Gatehouse** built by Wolsey and flanked with wings in the reign of Henry VIII.

♦ **Anne Boleyn's Gateway**, so-called as it was embellished by Henry VIII during her brief reign.

♦ **Clock Court** owes its name to the astronomical clock made for Henry VIII in 1540.

♦ **Gardens★★★** include the **Knot Garden**, **Privy Garden**, and **Maze** *(see Parks and Gardens).*

MUST SEE

TOWER OF LONDON ★★★

⊖ *Tower Hill. 0844 482 7777.*
www.hrp.org.uk. Open Mar–Oct
Tue–Sat 9am–5.30pm, Sun–
Mon 10am–5.30pm; Nov–Feb
Tue–Sat 9am–4.30pm, Sun–Mon
10am–4.30pm; last admission 30
min before closing. Closed Dec
24–26, Jan 1. £22 (£20.90 online).
Advance booking recommended
high season. Twilight tours winter
select dates, 7pm–8.30pm. £25.

Established by William I (the
Conqueror) after the Norman
Conquest, the reputation of the
Tower rests mainly on its role as
a prison and place of execution
for traitors. Unwilling inmates
have included Richard II, the Little
Princes, Edward V, and Richard of
York, who, according to legend,
were murdered here, Thomas More,
Anne Boleyn, Lady Jane Grey, Sir
Walter Raleigh, Guy Fawkes, Roger
Casement, and Rudolf Hess.

The 40 **Yeoman Warders** who
guard the Tower wear Tudor
uniforms and may be seen on
parade in the Inner Ward *(daily
at 11am)*. The Warders also give
guided tours *(1hr; from the
Middle Tower; no charge)* and
the **Ceremony of the Keys**, the
ceremonial closing of the Main
Gates, takes place each night
*(at 10.05pm; admission on written
application only)*.

Don't miss:

♦ **Traitor's Gate** (13C) Once used
to deliver enemies of the Crown
unseen by prying eyes.

♦ **Medieval Palace** Used by many
medieval kings and queens
during their frequent visits.

♦ **Bloody Tower** Traditionally the
place where the Little Princes
were murdered; its longest and

White Tower

most famous "resident" was
Sir Walter Raleigh.

♦ **White Tower** ★★★ Begun in
1078 by William I and completed
by William Rufus, this stone
fortress houses the **Chapel of
St John the Evangelist** ★★
(entrance from south side)
and the **Royal Armouries
Collection**, which includes
Henry VIII's suit of armor
(see For Kids).

♦ **Tower Green** The notorious
site of executions, including
Anne Boleyn.

♦ **Chapel Royal of St Peter ad
Vincula** Consecrated in the 12C,
with a fine Tudor font.

♦ **Beauchamp Tower** With walls
that reveal the graffiti of former
prisoners.

♦ **Jewel House** ★★★ Guards the
Crown Jewels—the crowns,
orbs, and rings that are the
priceless symbols of British
monarchy and include some
of the world's most famous
diamonds.

♦ **East Wall Walk** Explore the
massive defensive inner curtain
wall and the four towers.

ROYAL LONDON

73

- **The Ravens** Legend has it that the kingdom will fall if the ravens ever leave the Tower.

WINDSOR CASTLE★★★

Rail: from Waterloo or Paddington. Windsor. 020 7766 7304. www. royalcollection.org.uk. Open daily 9.45am–5.15pm (Nov–Feb 4.15pm); last admission 1hr 15min before closing. Allow 2.5–3hrs. £18.50, £10 when State Apartments closed.

Changing of the Guard★★★
Apr–Jul Mon–Sat 11am; Aug–Mar alternate days. Off map.

The oldest royal residence to have remained in continuous use, and the largest castle in England, Windsor's rich history spans almost 1,000 years. It has been the home of 39 monarchs and was the childhood home of HRH The Princesses Elizabeth and Margaret during World War II. Since then it has remained the Royal Family's principal home.

Highlights

- **Round Tower** Built by Henry II in c 1170 as a defense tower, it now houses the Royal Archives *(closed to public)*.
- **State Apartments★★** Magnificently furnished with works of art from the Royal Collection, including paintings by Rembrandt, Rubens, Canaletto, and Gainsborough. The apartments, originally created by Charles II, were much altered by George IV. In 1992 fire damaged more than 100 rooms at the Castle. The restoration work, completed in 1997, is a testament to the skills of the finest craftsmen.
- **Queen Mary's Dolls' House** One of the most famous dolls' house in the world.
- **St George's Chapel★★★** *01753 865 538.* The spiritual headquarters of England's prime order of chivalry, the Most Noble Order of the Garter, is also the final resting place of ten sovereigns including Charles I, brought here after his execution at Whitehall in 1649.
- **Albert Memorial Chapel** With a richly decorated interior.
- **Frogmore House** *Open May & Aug, certain days.* Set in the private Home Park, it was built in 1684 and today is furnished largely with possessions accumulated by Queen Mary.
- **Windsor Great Park★** – *See Parks and Gardens.*

Windsor Castle

View of Buckingham Palace from the lake in St James's Park

British Tourist Authority

BUCKINGHAM PALACE★★

⊖ *Green Park; St James's Park; Victoria. The Mall. 020 7766 7300. www.royalcollection.org.uk. Open late Jul–late Sept daily 9.30am–6.30/7.30pm (last admission 2hr 15min before closing). Timed ticket £21; combined Royal Day Out ticket with Queen's Gallery & Royal Mews £34.50.*

The ceremonial heart of London, "Buck House" is a focal point for Londoners and visitors alike. State occasions reflect the pomp and circumstance associated with the sovereign and the palace is a congregation point when national events arouse strong emotions. The interior presents a suite of Edwardian-style state rooms, decorated with treasures from the Royal Collection, including Sèvres porcelain, 18C French clocks and furniture, royal portraits, fine sculptures, and chandeliers. In the **Queen's Gallery★★** *(see Great Galleries)* hang masterpieces from the Royal Collection. From the grounds, where garden parties are held in summer, there's a superb view of the west front of the palace.

The **Royal Mews★★**, built by Nash in the 1820s, house stables, harness rooms, and coach houses displaying royal carriages, including the gold State Coach (1762), which has been used at every coronation since 1820. An ever popular attraction is the **Changing of the Guard★★★** ceremony *(see For Kids)*, which takes place in the palace forecourt. On the south side of the parade ground are the **Wellington Barracks**, built in 1833. The **Guards Museum** *(Birdcage Walk, SW1; 020 7414 3428; www.armymuseums. org.uk; £3)* is devoted to the history of the Guards Regiments. The **Guards Chapel** *(open as museum, except some ceremonial days)*, was destroyed by a flying bomb in June 1944 and rebuilt in 1963.

The Royal flag

When the Queen is in residence the Royal Standard is flown. In flag protocol, it is supreme. It must only be flown from buildings where the Queen is present and it flies above any other flag including the British Union Flag (Union Jack). It never flies at half-mast.

ROYAL LONDON

BANQUETING HOUSE★★

⊖Westminster. Whitehall. 0844 482 7777. www.hrp.org.uk. Open (government functions permitting, check by phone) Mon–Sun 10am–5pm (last admission 4.15pm). Closed public holidays, Dec 24– Jan 5. £6.60 (£6.05 online).

This Palladian-style hall is all that remains of Whitehall Palace, built by Inigo Jones for James I and destroyed by fire in 1698. Charles I commissioned the sumptuous painted ceiling by Rubens in 1629 and stepped out onto the scaffold in Whitehall through one of the hall's windows on January 30, 1649. Some 11 years later, Charles II received the Lords and Commons in the hall on the eve of his restoration. Although the building was used as a chapel and a museum from the 18C to the 20C, it now looks as splendid as it might have done in the 17C. The hall still serves superbly, beneath its flamboyant painted and gilded ceiling and sparkling chandeliers,

as a venue for the occasional official function.

KENSINGTON PALACE★★

⊖High St Kensington; Queensway. 0844 482 7777. ww.hrp.org.uk. Open daily Mar–Oct 10am–6pm (last admission 5pm); Nov–Feb 10am–5pm (last admission 4pm). £16.50 (£15.40 online).

Since its purchase in 1689 by William III, Kensington Palace has passed through three phases: the monarch's private residence with Wren as principal architect; a royal palace; and, since 1760, a residence for members of the royal family, notably Princess Victoria and the late Diana, Princess of Wales. It also became the home, in 1982, to the **Royal Ceremonial Dress Collection** (*currently closed to the public*), a priceless and fascinating national archive that documents the evolution of court dress, including pieces from the wardrobes of Diana, Princess of Wales, and the Queen.

The **State Apartments** are approached via the magnificent Queen's Staircase, designed by Wren (1691). Don't miss:

♦ **The Queen's Apartments** The private and intimate apartments of Queen Mary II.

♦ **The King's Apartments** Include the **Privy Chamber**, the colorful **Presence Chamber**, the **King's Grand Staircase** (Wren, 1689), with its walls and ceiling covered with trompe-l'œil paintings, and the **King's Gallery**. The 19C **Victorian Rooms** boast the **Cupola Room**, where Queen Victoria was baptized and the **Red Saloon** where she held her first Privy Council in1837.

Rubens ceiling, Banqueting House

©Historic Royal Palaces

QUEEN'S HOUSE★★

⊖ *North Greenwich. Rail: from Charing Cross; Waterloo. Greenwich. 020 8858 4422. www. nmm.ac.uk. Open daily 10am–5pm (last admission 4.30pm). No charge.* This Palladian villa (1616), now part of the National Maritime Museum, was England's first Classical building. Designed by Inigo Jones for the wives of James I and Charles I, the interior is fitted out in the style of the 1660s with a mixture of original and replica furnishings.

ST JAMES'S PALACE★★

⊖ *Green Park; St James's Park. The Mall. Palace not open to public. For security reasons, access to this area is severely restricted.* In 1532 the "goodly manor" built by Henry VIII was converted into a palace. Many royals have been born or died here: Charles I spent the night before his execution in the guardroom in 1649. When Whitehall Palace burned down in 1698, St James's became the chief royal residence. Today it is the official residence of the Princess Royal.

Clarence House – *Entrance on north side of The Mall. 020 7766 7303. www.royalcollection.org.uk. Guided tours Aug Mon–Fri 10am–4pm, Sat–Sun 10am–5.30pm. £9.50. Advance booking only.* The distinctive white stucco mansion—former home of the Queen Mother and now residence of the Prince of Wales and Duchess of Cornwall— was built in 1825 for the future William IV. The tour takes in five rooms used for official functions, displaying the Queen Mother's collection of 20C British art.

Queen's Chapel★ – *Entrance in Marlborough Rd.* Intended for the Infanta Maria of Spain but completed in 1625 by Inigo Jones for Charles I's eventual queen, Henrietta Maria, this was the first church in England to be designed completely outside the Perpendicular Gothic tradition.

ELTHAM PALACE★

Rail: Eltham or Mottingham from London Bridge. 020 8294 2548. www.elthampalace.org.uk. Open Sun–Thu 10am–6pm (Nov–Feb Sun 10am–4pm). See map p 101. £10.20. Once owned by Odo, Bishop of Bayeux and half-brother of William the Conqueror, the first monarch to live here was Edward II. Edward IV added the **Great Hall** in 1480. The palace gradually fell into ruins and was abandoned during the late 18C and 19C. In 1931, it was leased to Sir Stephen Courtauld, who restored the Great Hall and built his own beautiful Art Deco country home **Courtauld House**. The palace is approached over a stone bridge straddling the moat and has fine landscaped **gardens**.

Westminster Hall★ – *See City of Westminster, p 25.*

©English Heritage Photo Library
Eltham Palace

MAJOR MUSEUMS

From ancient to innovative, grand to eclectic, London's museum culture is world class. Start with the largest, such as the British, Victoria and Albert, Science, and Natural History Museums, for a taste of the sheer scale and quality of the national collections. The Science Museum takes a cutting-edge look at the scientific discoveries and questions of our age, while the Imperial War Museum explores some compelling social stories, even for those with no real interest in miltary history.

BRITISH MUSEUM★★★

⊖Tottenham Court Rd; Russell Sq; Holborn. Great Russell St. 020 7323 8181. www.britishmuseum.org. Open daily 10am–5.30pm (Fri 8.30pm). No charge.

The British Museum is undoubtedly one of the finest museums in the world, and its stunning treasures represent a vast canvas of the history of civilization. The **Great Court** has been transformed from an open, gloomy courtyard to the largest covered square in Europe. Its soaring glass-and-steel roof, spanning the space to the circular **Reading Room** (1857), is an architectural marvel, designed by Sir Norman Foster. The **King's Library**, built in 1827 to house the library of George III, now houses an exhibition discovering the world of the 18C.

Highlights include:

- **Parthenon (Elgin) Marbles** From the Acropolis in Athens.
- **Mausoleum of Halikarnassos** One of the Seven Wonders of the World.
- **The Portland Vase** A famous Roman cameo-glass vessel.
- **The Sutton Hoo Ship Burial** Shows the rich variety of artifacts retrieved from an Anglo-Saxon royal tomb in Suffolk.
- **The Lewis Chessmen** Eighty pieces (mid-12C) carved from walrus ivory that were found in 1831 in the Outer Hebrides.
- **The Rosetta Stone** Part of an inscribed block of black basalt, which enabled scholars to decipher Egyptian hieroglyphs.
- **Egyptian Mummies** Displayed in gilded and painted cases, as well as mummified animals.
- **Hoa Hakananai'a** A huge moai from Easter Island.

Great Court, British Museum

Y. Kanazawa/Michelin

IMPERIAL WAR MUSEUM★★★

⊖ *Lambeth North. Lambeth Rd. 020 7416 5000. www.iwm.org.uk. Open daily 10am–6pm. No charge (except for some special exhibitions).*

The museum in no sense glorifies war, but honors those who served and looks at the social history surrounding British wars from 1914 to the present day. Two British 15-inch naval guns, used in World War II, command the main gate.

Imperial War Museum

©Imperial War Museum

Don't miss:

♦ **First World War Galleries**
Exploring the complex sequence of events that led to the conflict, as well as life in the trenches and at home.

♦ **Second World War Galleries**
Covering all aspects of the war, including the **Blitz Experience**, the Battle of Britain, the war at sea, and the home front.

♦ **Secret War** A compelling exhibition detailing the clandestine world of Britain's spy network.

♦ **Holocaust Exhibition** Recalling this somber part of history, from the rise of the Nazi party to the concentration camps *(children under 11 not admitted; not recommended for under 16s).*

Lord Monty

Bernard Montgomery (1887–1976) led the Allies to victory at the Battle of El Alamein (1942), one of the turning points of World War II. His documents and medals show how he became one of the great battlefield commanders.

NATIONAL MARITIME MUSEUM★★★

⊖ *North Greenwich. 020 8858 4422. www.nmm.ac.uk. Open daily 10am–5pm (Thu 8pm, last admission 30min before closing). No charge (except for some exhibitions). See map p 101.*

A fabulous collection of all things maritime (fine art, rare instruments, treasures, and mementoes) is displayed by this beautifully organized museum.

The development of Britain as a sea power is traced from Henry VIII's Tudor fleet through Captain Cook's travels in the South Seas to Sir John Franklin's Polar exploration. Themes include **Explorers**, **Passengers** (the age of the great cruise liners), **Planet Ocean**, **Maritime London**, and **Atlantic Worlds,** covering settlement in America and the development of the trans-Atlantic slave trade and its abolition. Nelson's military campaigns are illustrated with paintings, uniforms, logs, and maps, while his personal artifacts include his bullet-pierced uniform worn at Trafalgar.

79

SCIENCE MUSEUM★★★

⊖*South Kensington.*
Exhibition Rd. 0870 870 4868.
*www.sciencemuseum.org.uk. Open
daily 10am–6pm (last admission
5.15pm). No charge (except for
special exhibitions).*

The spirit of the Science Museum,
laid out over seven floors, is to
encourage initiative and reception
in learning and education by
presentation, exploration, and
explanation. There are innumerable
exhibits, constantly updated
"Science Boxes", countless working
models, and interactive computer
terminals, while helpful assistants
are on hand throughout the
galleries.

For a quick tour:

- **The Secret Life of the Home**
  Explains the development of the
  everyday household appliances
  that we take for granted.
- **Exploring Space** Boasts a full-
  sized replica of the *Eagle* lander
  that took Armstrong and Aldrin
  to the Moon in 1969.
- **The Challenge of Materials**
  Explains the various uses of
  state-of-the-art materials in the
  modern world. A spectacular
  glass bridge spans the gallery.

- **Making the Modern World**
  Some 150 exhibits mark the
  development of the modern
  industrial world from 1750 to
  the present day.
- **Fly 360°** Fly your own jet in
  this state-of-the-art simulator
  (*£12 for two*).
- **Flight** Displaying an
  extraordinary collection of
  aircraft.

Recommended for children:

- **The Garden** A series of
  interactive exhibits that make
  science fun.
- **Pattern Pod** Encourages
  children to study patterns in
  recurring events.
- **IMAX cinema** One of two IMAX
  screens in London; wide variety
  of films (*0870 870 4868*).
- **Antenna** Constantly updated,
  an exhibition devoted to
  science news.
- **Who am I?** Where visitors can
  morph their face to any age
  using computers.
- **Energy Gallery** Allows children
  to think critically about energy.
- **Launchpad** Where kids explore
  their environment through
  more than 50 interactive
  exhibits.

Making the Modern World

©Science Museum

VICTORIA AND ALBERT MUSEUM (V&A)★★★

⊖ *South Kensington. Cromwell Rd. 020 7942 2000. www.vam. ac.uk. Open daily 10am–5.45pm (Fri 10pm). No charge (except for special exhibitions).*

The Victoria and Albert Museum is a treasure trove of art objects and is Britain's National Museum of Art and Design. Masterpieces from all over the world create a wonderful hub of decorative arts. The museum is divided into four broad themes: Asia; Europe; Materials and Techniques; and Modern.

Asia – These rooms include Asian sculpture, illuminated Mughal manuscripts, oriental carpets, Chinese porcelain, and Japanese ceramics and paintings.

Europe – The galleries display medieval and Renaissance art, rich ivory carvings, stained glass, and metalwork. The **British Galleries** house the Great Bed of Ware, made of carved oak and mentioned by Shakespeare, as well as furniture by Chippendale and Pugin. The **Cast Courts** illustrate European sculpture through the centuries by way of plaster casts.

Materials & Techniques – Perhaps the richest part of the collection, it includes the **Fashion Gallery**, which charts the development of clothing since the 16C, and **Textiles**, spanning 5,000 years, with linens found in Egyptian tombs to the designs of William Morris. The impressive collection of **paintings** includes works by Constable and Turner as

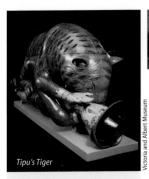

Tipu's Tiger

Victoria and Albert Museum

Tipu's Revenge

Tipu's Tiger was originally made for Tipu, Sultan of Mysore. The automaton represents a tiger mauling a British officer and contains a miniature organ that simulates the tiger's roar as well as the groans of its victim. Captured in 1799 at the fall of Seringapatam, it became a favorite exhibit in the East India Company's London museum.

well as *The Daydream* by Dante Gabriel Rossetti. The **Theatre & Performance** gallery focuses on the process of performance, including Pete Townsend's smashed Les Paul Gibson guitar and Adam Ant's Prince Charming costume. The silver and jewelry collections are also impressive.

Modern – These rooms show the influence of Modernism throughout the 20C on the design of furniture and everyday objects.

Don't miss – The café, located in the V&A's original **Morris, Gamble, and Poynter Rooms**, and the **John Madejski Garden**, a tranquil Italianate courtyard.

MAJOR MUSEUMS

WALLACE COLLECTION★★★

⊖ *Baker St. Manchester Sq. 020 7563 9500. www.wallace collection.org. Open daily 10am–5pm. No charge.*

This collection, started by the 1st Marquess of Hertford (1719–94), was bequeathed to the nation by the widow of Sir Richard Wallace, the 4th Marquess' son (1818–90). The striking exhibits include Sèvres porcelain, fine furniture, gold snuff boxes, tapestries, and armor, but perhaps the most breathtaking items on display are the paintings.

Laughing Cavalier (1624) by Frans Hals

Highlights include:

♦ **The Dining Room**, displaying two paintings by Canaletto.

♦ **The State Rooms**, hung with portraits by Joshua Reynolds and furnished with fine French furniture and porcelain.

♦ **The Gold Box Corridor**, a collection of gold snuff boxes, enameled or set with gems.

♦ **The Armories** houses a comprehensive range of weapons and armor from 10C–16C.

♦ **The Great Gallery**, with masterworks by Titian, Velázquez, Rembrandt, Gainsborough, and Rubens. Probably the museum's most famous painting is *The Laughing Cavalier* by Frans Hals.

NATURAL HISTORY MUSEUM★★

⊖ *South Kensington. Exhibition Rd/ Cromwell Rd. 020 7942 5000. www.nhm.ac.uk. Open daily 10am–5.50pm. No charge (except for some exhibitions).*

Dominating the Cromwell Road, the museum is housed in a fine Victorian Gothic revival building. Opened in 1881, after more than a century, the museum remains one of the most renowned centers for biological study in the world.

The Blue Zone – Includes the **Dinosaurs** gallery, the **Fishes, Amphibians and Reptiles** gallery, and the **Human Biology** gallery, with its interactive displays. A huge blue whale dominates the **Mammals** gallery.

The Green Zone – Includes insects, fossils, birds, and primates. The **Ecology** gallery traces the impact of man on the planet. The **Minerals** gallery displays gemstones, while the **Vault** at the end displays some valuable treasures, including the Nakla Martian meteorite and the Devonshire Emerald.

The Red Zone – The **Earth Hall** demonstrates how earthquakes and volcanoes harness the power of nature. The **Restless Surface** gallery examines how rock formations transform and shape our planet, and the **Earth's Treasury** displays specimens of gemstones, rocks, and minerals. **Earth Today and**

MUST SEE

©Wallace Collection

The World's Largest Cocoon

The Darwin Centre, an eight-story concrete cocoon in a glass atrium, houses over 20 million insect and plant specimens. Visitors can watch scientists working on research in modern laboratories and partake in interactive exhibitions.

Tomorrow looks at the importance of sustainable development to man and the planet.

The Orange Zone – Incorporates the **Darwin Centre** (open 10am–5.50pm) and the **Wildlife Garden** (open Apr–Oct), located on the West lawn outside the museum.

MUSEUM OF LONDON★★

⊖Barbican; St Paul's; Moorgate. 150 London Wall. 020 7001 9844. www.museumoflondon.org.uk. Open daily 10am–6pm. No charge.

This museum comprehensively and entertainingly tells of London's turbulent history from 1066 to the present day. Exhibits include the best Roman wall painting in Britain and sculptures from the **Temple of Mithras**, a Roman temple uncovered in the City in 1954 (Temple Court, Queen Victoria St), a model of the Rose Theatre based on archeological evidence, the Cheapside Hoard of Jacobean jewelry, a diorama of the Great Fire, the doors from Newgate Gaol, 19C shops and interiors, the Lord Mayor's Coach, souvenirs of the women's suffrage movement, the 1930s elevators from Selfridge's department store, and the excellent **World City** gallery exploring London's present identity and future. It also has an excellent branch museum: the **Museum in Docklands★** (see p 64).

NATIONAL ARMY MUSEUM★

⊖Sloane Sq. Royal Hospital Rd, Chelsea. 020 7730 0717. www. nam.ac.uk. Open daily 10am–5.30pm, closed for redevelopment until summer 2016. No charge.

Visit the National Army Museum and find out how Britain's past helped shape its present and future.

The major exhibition examines more than three decades of action on the world stage by the modern British army, the conflicting interests of enforcing peace through violent means, balancing global security with the needs of vulnerable communities and the demands of the job on the personal lives of our troops.

What's On – The museum offers a program of events, including lunchtime lectures and celebrity speakers and will be marking the centenary of World War I in 2014 and the bicentenary of the Battle of Waterloo in 2015.

A two-year redevelopment program is currently in process, visit www.nam.ac.uk/microsites/future/ for updates.

Viking weapons, Museum of London

©Museum of London

GREAT GALLERIES

The roots of many of London's collections lie in the bequests of 18C and 19C collectors, such as Henry Tate (Tate Britain), while others have evolved through necessity or resourcefulness; in the 20C, the outstandingly successful Tate Modern was created in a former power station in Bankside, for example. With so many galleries to visit in London, you'll be hard pressed to see even a fraction of them. The national galleries have vast permanent collections, constantly invigorated by temporary exhibitions. Many major galleries are subsidized and free to visit, carrying on an ingrained tradition of culture; however, donations are appreciated.

NATIONAL GALLERY★★★

⊖ *Charing Cross. Trafalgar Sq. 020 7747 2885. www.national gallery.org.uk. Open daily 10am–6pm (Fri 9pm). Closed Jan 1, Dec 24–26. No charge (except for special exhibitions).*

Founded in 1824 by parliamentary purchase, the National Gallery moved to its present majestic building designed by William Wilkins and overlooking Trafalgar Square in 1838. Rambling through a large museum is both exhilarating and exhausting.

If you are pressed for time, choose a favorite period in history, locate it on the gallery floor plan *(free from entrance foyers)* and explore the art of the times. Browsing will allow you to discover unfamiliar images and perhaps provide you with some new "favorites."

Highlights include:

- ◆ Leonardo's cartoon of *The Virgin and Child with St Anne and John the Baptist.*
- ◆ Holbein's *The Ambassadors* (stand to the right to view the distorted skull).
- ◆ Rembrandt's *Self Portrait.*
- ◆ The **British School** of portrait and landscape painting, including Turner's *The Fighting Temeraire,* Constable's *The Hay Wain,* and Stubbs's *Whistlejacket.*
- ◆ The **Impressionist Collection**, including Seurat's *Bathers at Asnières* and Monet's *Bathers at La Grenouillère.*
- ◆ Van Gogh's *Sunflowers.*

National Gallery

© National Gallery, London

Tate Britain

©Ming Tang Evans/APA Publications

TATE BRITAIN★★★

⊖ *Pimlico. Milbank. 0207 887 8888 (booking & info). www.tate.org.uk/britain. Open daily 10am–6pm, last admission 5.15pm. No charge (except for some special exhibitions). Closed Dec 24–26.*

Fifty years after the founding of the National Gallery (1824), the nation had acquired a large number of works that had no permanent home. In 1889, the sugar broker Henry Tate, an astute collector of British art, offered his collection of paintings to the nation together with £80,000 for a purpose-built gallery dedicated to British art on condition that the government provide a site for it. The Tate opened in 1897 in a superb waterfront setting overlooking the Pimlico riverside. This bright, imposing building is a splendid showcase for British Art from 1500 to the present day, and after extensive redevelopment, boasts modern facilities for innovative displays of its fine collections. The gallery has a strong tradition of well-presented special exhibitions and public events; it also sponsors The Turner Prize, a prestigious, if always controversial, award for the visual arts.

Don't miss:

♦ Nicholas Hilliard's miniature of *Queen Elizabeth I*.
♦ Hogarth's *A Scene from 'The Beggar's Opera' VI*.
♦ The portraits by Reynolds and Gainsborough.
♦ The paintings of John Constable, including *Flatford Mill*.
♦ The works of the Pre-Raphaelites, in particular Millais's *Ophelia* and *Christ in the House of his Parents*, Rossetti's *Ecce Ancilla Domini*, and Holman Hunt's *The Ship* and *The Awakening Conscience*.
♦ The works of the American-born artist Whistler and John Singer Sargent.
♦ The **Clore Gallery** entirely devoted to Turner.
♦ The modern age represented by the YBAs (Young British Artists), such as Damien Hirst, Tracey Emin, and Marc Quinn.

COURTAULD GALLERY ★★

⊖ *Temple; Charing Cross; Covent Garden. Somerset House, Strand. 020 7848 2526. www.courtauld. ac.uk/gallery. Open daily 10am–6pm (last admission 5.30pm), Dec 24 10am–4pm. £6, £3 Mon (including public holidays).*

This fine collection includes recognized masterpieces from a wide range of periods stretching from the Gothic to Modernism. The works are grouped by benefactor to give a clearer idea of the mind of each collector.

Gallery 1 – Thomas Gambier-Parry (1816–88) collection of 14C Italian Primitives.

Galleries 2–4 – Samuel Courtauld's collection of Impressionist and Post-Impressionist paintings. Highlights include: Cézanne's *The Lac d'Annecy*, Seurat's *The Bridge at Courbevoie*, Monet's *Autumn Effect at Argenteuil*, Renoir's *La Loge*, Monet's *Antibes*, Manet's *A Bar at the Folies-Bergère*, his last major work, Gauguin's *Te Rerioa*, Van Gogh's *Self-portrait with Bandaged Ear*, and Modigliani's *Female Nude*.

Gallery 5 – Viscount Lee of Fareham's collection of Italian Renaissance paintings, including Botticelli's *Holy Trinity* and Giovanni Bellini's *Assassination of St Peter Martyr*.

Galleries 6–7 – Houses the Princes' Gate Collection, focusing on Rubens and the Venetian sources of his ceiling paintings. There are also works by Pieter Bruegel the Elder, Tiepolo, William Dobson, Sir Peter Lely, Gainsborough, Reynolds, Raeburn, and Romney.

Gallery 8 – Displays paintings and bronzes by Degas and works by Toulouse-Lautrec.

Galleries 9–14 – 20C collections including Matisse (*Woman in a Kimono*) and Fauvism.

Galleries 11a and 11b – The Roger Fry Collection—contemporary works by Duncan Grant, Vanessa Bell, and Walter Sickert.

Gallery 12 – Devoted to a series of drawings and prints.

Galleries 13–14 – Expressionist Art and Modernism.

Gallery 15 – Temporary exhibitions.

Detail of A Bar at the Folies-Bergères *(1882) by Edouard Manet*

Samuel Courtauld Trust, The Courtauld Gallery, London

National Portrait Gallery

©Colin Streater/National Portrait Gallery

NATIONAL PORTRAIT GALLERY★★

⊖Leicester Sq; Charing Cross. St Martin's Pl. 020 7306 0055. www.npg.org.uk. Open daily 10am–6pm (Thu–Fri 9pm). Closed Dec 24–26. No charge (except for special exhibitions).

The fascination of portraits of the great and the good who have wielded power or made a significant contribution to British society throughout the centuries is irresistible as the historic panorama unfolds. Wander through the gallery at leisure and enjoy a meal in the rooftop restaurant *(booking recommended; 020 7312 2490)*, from which there are wonderful views.

Founded in 1856, the National Collection moved to its present location behind the National Gallery in 1896. Today, over 5,000 personalities represent a rich history of Britain. The permanent collection is presented in chronological order from the top down.

- ◆ **The Tudor Galleries** – include Holbein's sketch of Henry VIII with his father Henry VII, Mary I, and several portraits of Elizabeth I and her favorites.
- ◆ **The 17C** – Contains the Chandos Portrait, arguably

the most famous of William Shakespeare. It also has portraits of Charles I, Oliver Cromwell, and Charles II and his mistress Nell Gwynne.

- ◆ **Georgian and Regency** – The Arts and Sciences are reflected by portraits of Wren, Reynolds, and Sir Hans Sloane, as well as heros like Nelson and the Duke of Wellington. Romantic writers are represented by Wordsworth, Coleridge, Burns, and Lord Byron.
- ◆ **The Victorians** – As well as portraits of Queen Victoria and Prince Albert, the **Statesmen's Gallery** contains portraits and busts of political figures, and there are personalities such as Florence Nightingale, Alfred Tennyson, Charles Dickens, and Isambard K Brunel.
- ◆ **The 20C** – The great figures of the century include Churchill, Virginia Woolf, Laurence Olivier, and Alexander Fleming. The **Balcony Gallery** (1960–90), has portraits of the royal family, Alec Guinness, Paul McCartney, and Margaret Thatcher. **Britain since 1990** includes icons such as Richard Branson, Ken Loach, and Stephen Hawking.

Lord Byron (1813) by Thomas Phillips

© National Portrait Gallery, London

GREAT GALLERIES

87

QUEEN'S GALLERY★★

⊖*Victoria; Green Park; Hyde Park Corner. Buckingham Palace. 020 7766 7301. www.royalcollection. org.uk. Open daily 10am–5.30pm, last admission 4.30pm. £9.75.*

The Queen's Gallery at Buckingham Palace is a permanent space dedicated to changing exhibitions of items from the magnificent Royal Collection, which includes Holbein watercolors, Canaletto paintings, fine furniture, sculpture, porcelain and ceramics, and silver and gold plate.

TATE MODERN★★

⊖*Southwark; St Paul's. 020 7887 8888. www.tate.org.uk/modern. Open daily 10am–6pm (Fri–Sat 10pm), last admission 45min before closing. No charge.*
*The **Tate Boat** runs every 40min between Tate Modern and Tate Britain, daily during gallery opening times. £6.80, £12 return. www.thamesclippers.com.*

The former Bankside Power Station has been converted to house the Tate Gallery's collections of international 20C art. The museum is split into seven levels. On level one is the **Turbine Hall**, which hosts vast commissions

Touring Tip

Visiting the Queen's Gallery

Pre-booking for the Queen's Gallery is strongly advised. A small number of tickets is held back for sale on the day, which are available from the Gallery's ticket desks from 9.30am on a strictly first come, first served basis and are for one of the timed admissions for that day only.

by different artists every six months. On levels three and five are the museum collections that are rotated according to various themes. Level four is devoted to special exhibitions.

The collections include modern masters such as Cézanne, Seurat, Van Gogh, Matisse, and Picasso. There are also works by Cubists, such as Braque and Léger, while Dada and Surrealism are represented by Duchamp, Magritte, Dalí, and Joan Miro. Futurism, German Expressionism, Abstraction, and Pop Art are also on display, with artists such as Francis Bacon, Jackson Pollock, Roy Lichtenstein, and Andy Warhol all represented.

Imposing mass of Tate Modern, Millennium Bridge

Pawel Libera/VisitLondon

MUST SEE

HAYWARD GALLERY

⊖ *Waterloo. Southbank Centre. 020 7960 4200. www.hayward gallery.org.uk. Open daily 10am–6pm (Thu–Fri 8pm).*

The gallery, purpose-built to house major temporary exhibitions of paintings and sculpture, opened in 1968. The building, a terrace-like concrete structure, has five large gallery spaces and three open-air sculpture courts on two levels.

ICA (INSTITUTE OF CONTEMPORARY ARTS)

⊖ *Charing Cross; Piccadilly Circus. The Mall. 020 7930 3647. www.ica.org.uk. Galleries: Open Tue–Sun 11am–6pm (Thu 9pm). No charge.*

This not-for-profit, multi-disciplinary arts center was established in 1947 by a collective of artists, poets, and writers to explore contemporary culture. The ICA, housing two galleries, two cinemas, a theater, and a reading room, has presented some of the most radical exhibitions, movies, and music, and remains a dedicated space for new, experimental, and independent artists.

ROYAL ACADEMY OF ARTS

⊖ *Piccadilly Circus. Burlington House, Piccadilly. 020 7300 8000 (info). www.royalacademy.org.uk. Open daily 10am–6pm (Fri 10pm). Exhibitions £8–12.*

The Royal Academy, founded in 1768, is the oldest fine arts institution in Britain. It hosts some of the capital's finest exhibitions, including the annual Summer Exhibition.The **Sackler Galleries**, designed by Sir Norman Foster,

opened in 1991. The academy's treasures, on display in the **John Madeski Fine Rooms**, include paintings by Reynolds, Gainsborough, Constable, and Turner, as well as 18C furniture, Queen Victoria's paintbox, Michelangelo's unfinished marble Madonna and Child, and the famous copy of da Vinci's *Last Supper*.

SAATCHI GALLERY

⊖ *Sloane Sq. Duke of York's HQ, Sloane Sq. 020 7823 2363. www.saatchigallery.com. Open daily 10am–6pm. No charge.*

Opened at its new location in 2008, this cutting-edge interactive art gallery showcases contemporary art by largely unseen young British artists or established international artists unknown in Britain. The vast space with its abundance of natural light holds temporary exhibitions; the **Project Room** is a space for artists featured in the collection, but not in the main exhibition program. The gallery operates a free entry policy to all shows and exhibitions.

White Cube Gallery

Set up by Jay Jopling in 1993 on Duke St, this contemporary art gallery moved to larger premises in Hoxton Square (now closed) before White Cube Mason's Yard opened in 2006 (⊖ *Piccadilly Circus*) and White Cube Bermondsey in 2011 (⊖ *London Bridge*). The galleries stage high profile exhibitions of work by leading international and British artists. (*020 7930 5373, whitecube.com*).

PARKS AND GARDENS

London is blessed with many beautiful green spaces. The royal parks are the city's green lungs, providing vast areas of open space for relaxation, recreation, and entertainment. Gardening is a national passion and landscaped gardens such as Hampton Court, Kew, Buckingham Palace, and Kensington Gardens provide a glorious show in all seasons.

HAMPTON COURT GARDENS★★★

Rail: Hampton Court from Waterloo. 0844 482 7777. www.hrp.org.uk. Gardens open daily Apr–Sept 10am–6pm; Oct–Mar 10am–5.30pm. House & gardens £18.20 (£17.05 online), gardens only £5.72. See map p 100.

The 60-acre (26ha) gardens bear the imprint of their creators: the Tudor, Stuart, and Orange monarchs, their designers, and great gardeners. Over the years features have changed in line with fashion but the gardens today represent a unique historical and horticultural resource of international value. *(For House see Royal London.)*

Don't miss:

- The **Privy Garden**, restored to its original layout of 1702.
- The **Knot Garden**, in its original walled Elizabethan site.

- The **Great Vine★**, planted in 1768 by Capability Brown for George III.
- The **Fountain Garden.**
- The **Tudor tiltyards**, surrounded by six observation towers, of which one remains, are now walled rose gardens.
- The **Maze**, begun in 1690 as a courtly entertainment for William II, boasts half a mile (0.8km) of winding paths with towering yew tree walls. It takes around 20 minutes to reach the center.

🚣 REGENT'S PARK★★★

⊖ *Regent's Park; Baker St.*

Bounded by Regent's Canal to the north, Regent's Park is surrounded by dazzling 17C **terraces★★** and villas. The superb amenities include a large **boating lake** *(boats for hire)*, tennis courts, and band music in summer. The Inner Circle contains **Queen Mary's Gardens**, a delightful haven; the romantic **Rose Garden** is filled with heady perfumes in summer. The **Open Air Theatre** *(0844 826 4242; www.openairtheatre.org)* stages a summer season of open-air performances of plays and musicals. Both young and old enjoy the attractions of **London Zoo★★** *(see For Kids)*. **Cruises** are available *(see Getting Around)* on the **Regent's Canal** *(towpath open 9am–dusk)* from cosmopolitan

Regent's Canal at St Johns Wood

Ricky Leaver / age fotostock

Glass house, Kew

Pawel Libera/VisitLondon

Little Venice *(Maida Vale)*, with its chic bars and cafés, to **Camden Lock**.

ROYAL BOTANIC GARDENS, KEW★★★

⊖ *Kew Gardens. 020 8332 5655. www.kew.org. Gardens: Open daily Mon–Fri 9.30am–6.30pm, Sat–Sun and public holidays 9.30am–7.30pm; Oct–Feb earlier closing; call or see website. Glasshouses, museum, and galleries close 30min earlier. See map p 100.*

Kew Gardens are pure pleasure—the color and architecture of the trees a delight in all seasons. This 300 acre/120ha garden is an offshoot of laboratories engaged in vital botanical research. The curatorship of the biggest herbarium in the world, a wood museum, a vast botanical library, and the training of student gardeners are also within its province. The site boasts listed buildings, glasshouses, galleries, and a museum. Declared a UNESCO World Heritage Site in 2003, these are probably the most important—if not the most beautiful—botanical gardens in the world.

Gardens – Landscaped by Capability Brown, the gardens today present a pleasant mix of lawns, formal gardens, and wooded areas, with typical 18C garden follies, including temples, a ruined arch, an **Orangery★**, and a **Pagoda★**.

Greenhouses – The iron- and-glass **Palm House★★** houses a range of tropical plants. **Temperate House★** epitomizes Victorian conservatory construction while the **Evolution House** recreates the climate of change affecting the Earth. **Alpine House** is a rock landscape including a refrigerated bed. The **Princess of Wales Tropical Conservatory** recreates ten different tropical habitats, from mangrove swamp to desert.

Galleries – The **Marianne North Gallery** exhibits paintings of plants, insects, and general scenes from the many countries Miss North visited between 1871 and 1884. The **Shirley Sherwood Gallery**, opened in 2008, is dedicated to botanical art, both historic and contemporary.

Houses and other buildings – **Kew Palace★★ (Dutch House)** A terracotta brick building (1631) built by Samuel Fortrey, a London Merchant of Dutch parentage. At the rear is the **Queen's Garden. Queen Charlotte's Cottage**, a "rustic" thatched house (1772), was designed by Queen Charlotte as a picnic house. The **Japanese Gateway**★ was imported for the Anglo-Japanese Exhibition of 1912.

QUEEN ELIZABETH OLYMPIC PARK★★★

⊖*Stratford; Stratford International; Hackney Wick. queenelizabeth olympicpark.co.uk.*

The Olympic Park, laid out for the London 2012 Olympic Games and reopened in spring 2014 as London's newest park, is 560 acres of woodland, waterways and grassland, dotted with sports venues such as the Aquatics Centre (designed by Zaha Hadid) and the 54,000 seater stadium. There are fountains, play areas, themed walkways and Anish Kapoor's **ArcelorMittal Orbit**★★, a 115-metre-high red twisted sculpture and viewing tower which affords fantastic views over London.

HYDE PARK AND KENSINGTON GARDENS★★

⊖*Marble Arch; Hyde Park Corner; Knightsbridge; Queensway; Lancaster Gate; Park La; Knightsbridge.*

The linked green expanses of Hyde Park and Kensington Gardens offer

year-round attractions. Every day people flock to the parks to walk their dogs, jog, ride, go boating, swim, skate, sail model boats, feed the ducks, or play sports. Concerts in the park also attract the crowds.

Hyde Park highlights:

♦ **Marble Arch**, a fine triumphal arch that stands on the site of the former Tyburn gallows.

♦ **Speakers' Corner**, where anyone may mount their soap box and address the crowds.

♦ **Queen Elizabeth Gate**, erected in 1993 to celebrate Queen Elizabeth, the late Queen Mother's 93rd birthday.

♦ **Wellington Arch** *020 7930 2726. www.english-heritage.org.uk.* The viewing platforms offer great views over the parks.

♦ **Hyde Park Barracks** from where the Guardsmen ride down to Horse Guards' when the Queen returns to London.

♦ **Hudson Bird Sanctuary**, where over 90 species have been recorded.

♦ **The Serpentine**, used for boating and swimming, with a children's paddling pool.

♦ **Diana Memorial Fountain** *Open Apr–Aug 10am–8pm; Sept 10am–7pm; Mar and Oct 10am–6pm; Nov–Feb 10am–4pm.* London's official memorial to Diana, Princess of Wales, who died tragically young in 1997.

Kensington Gardens

The former gardens of **Kensington Palace**★★ *(see Royal London)*, the remaining original features include the **Round Pond**, constructed facing the State Apartments, the **Broad Walk**, and the **Orangery**★. Later additions are the Edwardian

Aerial view of Kensington Gardens

Ricky Leaver / age fotostock

sunken garden, the statue of Peter Pan (1912), and Henry Moore's **The Arch** (1979).

The **Albert Memorial★** was commissioned by a heartbroken Queen Victoria on the death of her beloved husband Prince Albert (1872). The **Serpentine Gallery** (*Gallery Lawn; www.serpentinegallery.org; open Tue–Sun 10am–6pm*), a compact pavilion shaded by trees, stages exhibitions of modern art.

RICHMOND PARK★★

🚇 *Richmond. Rail: Richmond from Waterloo Station and by North London Line. See map p 100.*

The countryside had been a royal chase for centuries when Charles I enclosed 2,470 acres/494ha as a park in 1637. The largest of the royal parks, Richmond is famous for its herds of virtually tame deer, its majestic oaks, and the spring flowers of the Isabella Plantation. On a fine day from the top of the Henry VIII mound there is a panoramic **view★★★** extending from Windsor Castle to the dome of St Paul's. Among the houses in the park are **Pembroke Lodge**, adapted by John Soane from a molecatcher's cottage, and **White Lodge**, built by George II in 1727 as a hunting lodge and since 1955 used as the junior section of the Royal Ballet School. (*See also Excursions.*)

ST JAMES'S PARK★★

🚇 *St James's Park.*

London's oldest park is known for its flower borders, pelicans, and wildfowl on the lake. Henry VIII first acquired the park in 1532 as a hunting ground. James I later established a menagerie of animals and exotic birds here. Charles II

St James's Park

Prized Birds

St James's Park pelicans have a long-standing history: the first one, from Astrakhan, was a gift to Charles II given by a Russian ambassador—it promptly flew off and was shot over Norfolk. Peter from Karachi stayed 54 years before emigrating; no one knows where.

aligned aviaries along what came to be called Birdcage Walk and opened the park to the public. In the 19C Nash landscaped the park itself. Take a stroll by the lake or relax on the grass and enjoy band music. From the **Blue Bridge** there is a fine view of Buckingham Palace.

BLACKHEATH★

Rail: Blackheath from Cannon Street or London Bridge.

Blackheath has been used over the years as a rallying ground by rebel forces, including Wat Tyler (1381), the Kentishmen under Jack Cade (1450), and the Cornishmen under Audley (1497). In more joyful mood, in 1415 the people greeted Henry V here on his victorious return from Agincourt, in 1660 Charles II was welcomed by the Restoration Army, and in 1608, it is said, James I

PARKS AND GARDENS

93

taught the English to play golf on Blackheath. The heath is ringed by stately 18C and 19C **terraces** and **houses★**, when merchants, newly rich from the expanding docks, began to build in the vicinity.

VICTORIA EMBANKMENT GARDENS★

⊖*Embankment.*

This narrow strip of public park by the Thames was created in 1874 with the construction of the Embankment. The gardens contain a number of statues and monuments as well as the **York House Water-gate** (c 1626). Hire a deckchair and enjoy a summer lunchtime concert.

WINDSOR GREAT PARK★

Rail: Egham, Windsor, or Virginia Water from Waterloo or Paddington. 01753 860 222. www.theroyallandscape.co.uk. Open daily dawn–dusk.

This 4,800-acre/1,942ha park, once the hunting ground of Saxon chiefs and medieval knights, is today linked to **Windsor Castle★★★** *(see Royal London)* by the **Long Walk** (3mi/5km) planted by Charles II. Nestling in the park are two former royal residences: **Royal Lodge** and **Cumberland Lodge**. **Valley Gardens**, planted with shrubs and trees that extend to Virginia Water, is a 130-acre/53-ha area arranged around an artificial lake *(01784 435 544; open daily 10am–6pm, winter 4.30pm/dusk)*. The **Savill Garden** *(01784 435 544; open daily 10am–6pm, Nov–Feb 4.30pm)* is an independent, landscaped wooded garden laid out in 1932 and endowed with a fine **Temperate House** in 1995. It is a glorious show in the spring when the flowers burst into symphonies of color.

BATTERSEA PARK

Rail: Battersea Park from Victoria; Queenstown Road from Waterloo.

The marshy waste of Battersea Fields, popular with duelers in the 16C, had become ill-famed by the time Thomas Cubitt proposed that a park be laid out here in 1843. Today the park is one of London's most charming and interesting, with a boating lake, sculptures by Henry Moore and Barbara Hepworth, an adventure playground and children's petting zoo, cafés, and many sports facilities. The **Japanese Peace Pagoda** (1985) is one of several instituted by a world peace organization. Opposite the park, the familiar and iconic industrial landmark of **Battersea Power Station** lies derelict since its closure

Greenwich Park

Simon Kreitem/British Tourist Authority

in 1983. At present there are plans to convert it into a shopping and entertainment center.

CHELSEA PHYSIC GARDEN

⊖ *Sloane Sq. 66 Royal Hospital Rd. 020 7352 5646. www.chelseaphysic garden.co.uk. Open Apr–Oct Tue–Fri, Sun and public holidays 11am–6pm. £9.90.*

The botanical garden was founded in 1673 by the Worshipful Society of Apothecaries of London on land leased from Sir Hans Sloane; his statue stands in the center. The garden has a remarkable record: Georgia's cotton seeds came from the South Seas via the Physic Garden, India's tea from China, and Malaya's rubber from South America.

GREEN PARK

⊖ *Green Park.*

Covering 47 acres/19ha, Green Park is quite different from its neighbor St James's Park. It was created in 1667 by Charles II, who regularly came here in the early morning to walk up a path to what is now Hyde Park Corner—hence **Constitution Hill**. Peaceful, with mature trees and grassland, from the east side of the park there is a fine view of **Spencer House★★**.

GREENWICH PARK

⊖ *North Greenwich. See map p 101. See also* **Greenwich★★★**, *p 62.*

Greenwich Park is the oldest enclosed royal domain. It extends for 180 acres/73ha in a sweep of chestnut avenues and grass to a point 155ft/47m above the river crowned by the Royal Observatory and the General Wolfe monument. On the slope below the

Chelsea Physic Garden

The Phare

©Charlie Hopkinson

Observatory are traces of the 17C giant grass steps by Le Nôtre.

HAMPSTEAD HEATH

⊖ *Hampstead. See map p 100.*

Hampstead Heath was the common of Hampstead Manor, an area where washerwomen laid out their laundry to bleach in the 18C. Since early times it has been a popular place of recreation. **Whitestone Pond** and the milestone ("Holborn Bars 4½," located at the base of the aerial) from which it takes its name lie on London's highest ground (437ft/133m). *(See also Excursions.)*

HOLLAND PARK

⊖ *Holland Park. Open daily 8am–8pm (dusk in winter). Open-air opera Jun–Aug (0845 230 9769).*

One of the most peaceful and romantic parks in London, Holland Park boasts areas of semi-wild woodland, sports facilities, and formal gardens centered around the ruins of Holland House. In summer open-air performances of opera and dance are staged in the forecourt. Peacocks wander through the flower beds, water tinkles in the Japanese garden, and weddings are held in the charming orangery.

Wimbledon Common; Osterley Park★★; Syon Park★★ – *See Excursions.*

SPORTS LONDON

London boasts a number of Premier League and First Division football teams. Cricket was originally a British gentlemen's sport that was exported to the colonies to encourage team spirit, discipline, and sportsmanship. Wimbledon Tennis Championships are summer highlights. Rugby matches, especially the Six Nations Cup, are special events.

CRICKET

Lord's Cricket Ground –
St John's Wood. St John's Wood Rd, NW8 8QN. 020 7432 1000. www.lords.org. Tours daily (except match days, check website for timings).
London's main cricket ground and headquarters of several autonomous bodies: the International Cricket Council that supervises the game at international level; the Marylebone Cricket Club (MCC), founded in 1787, which set up the Test and County Cricket Board to administer international matches and the county game in the UK; and the Middlesex County Cricket Club, founded in 1877.

The Kia Oval – Oval.
Kennington Oval, Kennington, SE11 5SS. 0844 375 1845, www.kiaoval.com. www.surrey cricket.com. London's second cricket ground and home to the Surrey County Cricket Club.

FOOTBALL

Arsenal FC, Emirates Stadium –
Arsenal. Hornsey Rd, N7 7AJ. 020 7619 5003, www.arsenal.com. Tours daily (except match days). The Arsenal team are known as the "Gunners" because of the club's association with the former royal armaments factory.

Chelsea FC, Stamford Bridge –
Fulham Broadway. Fulham Rd, SW6 1HS. 0871 984 1955. www.chelseafc.com. Tours daily (except match days). One of London's most famous football clubs.

Tottenham FC, White Hart Lane –
Rail: White Hart Lane. 748 High Rd, N17 0AP. 0844 499 5000, www.tottenhamhotspur.com. Tours daily (except match days). Premier league club commonly refered to as "Spurs".

Emirates Stadium

©Arsenal Football Club

🏟 Wembley Stadium –
⊖Wembley Park. HA9 0WS.
0844 980 8001, www.wembley
stadium.com. Tours daily (except
match days).

The home of English football since
1923, the new Wembley Stadium
opened in spring 2007 and quickly
re-established itself as the country's
leading venue for sports and
entertainment events. With room
for up to 90,000 fans and state-
of-the-art facilities, the stadium
plays host to football showcase
events, home internationals, and
important rugby league events.
The stadium also hosts a diverse
range of additional sports, music,
and entertainment events
each year.

GREYHOUND RACING

Wimbledon Stadium – ⊖Tooting
Broadway; Wimbledon. Plough La,
SW17 0BL. 0870 840 8905.
www.lovethedogs.co.uk. £7.
Famous greyhound track with
regular meetings on Friday and
Saturday evenings.

POLO

Guards Polo Club – ⊖Egham.
Smith's Lawn, Windsor Great Park,
Englefield Green, TW20 0HP. 01784
434 212. www.guardspoloclub.com.
Matches played every Saturday and
Sunday at 3pm. In July the Cartier
International tournament is held
here, while the Ladies' National
Polo Championship is held at
Ascot Park (Sunningdale).

RUGBY

Harlequins Stoop Memorial
Ground – Rail: Twickenham.

Langhorn Dr, Twickenham/
Richmond, TW2 7SX. 0871 527
1315. www.quins.co.uk.
The ground of one of London's
premier rugby clubs, the
Harlequins.

Twickenham – Rail: Twickenham.
Rugby Rd, TW1 1DZ. 0870 405
2000. www.rfu.com.
Britain's finest rugby ground
and the headquarters of the
Rugby Football Union. Major
international matches are played
on Twickenham's hallowed turf,
including home games in the
Six Nations Tournament.
The **Museum of Rugby** features
the "Twickenham Experience":
a guided tour of 14 exhibition
rooms and the 50-year-old baths.

TENNIS

🏟 All-England Lawn Tennis Club –
⊖Wimbledon; Southfields.
Church Rd, SW19 5AE. 020 8944
1066. www.wimbledon.com.
Tours daily (except during the
Championships).

Home of the world's premier
tennis tournament, Wimbledon is
actually a private members' club—
the All England Lawn Tennis and
Croquet Club. The **museum** (020
8946 6131; open daily 10am–5pm,
during Championships 8pm), with
touch screens and interactive
displays, charts the history of
tennis and Wimbledon from its
earliest years. Tours take in the
museum, courts, players' facilities,
and broadcasting studios.
The All-England Championships,
first held in 1877, run for two
weeks from the end of June.
(See also Excursions).

EXCURSIONS

In order to enjoy some of London's most attractive locales, or just to escape the hurly-burly of the city center, a day trip to the leafy suburbs should be on every visitor's itinerary. To the west lie a plethora of beautiful districts such as Chiswick and Richmond, not to mention the royal palaces of Hampton Court and Windsor Castle *(see Royal London)*. To the north is Hampstead, with its affluent village, and to the south lies Wimbledon, famed for its annual tennis tournament.

KEW★

⊖*Kew Gardens.*
The Thames draws a great loop around Kew, an affluent residential area in west London with a village atmosphere. A day excursion brings the delight of strolling through the magnificent **Royal Botanic Gardens★★★** *(see Parks and Gardens).*

Waterlily House, Kew Gardens
D. Chapuis/MICHELIN

Kew Museum of Water and Steam – *Green Dragon La, Brentford. 020 8568 4757. www.kbsm.org. Open daily 11am–4pm. £11.50 (£10.35 online).* This museum shows the development of James Watt's basic idea to the Waddon Engine, the last steam-powered water pumping engine in commercial use. There are also traction engines, steam lorries, a narrow-gauge railway, a water-wheel (1702), and a forge.

Kew Green – The green is surrounded by attractive houses,

including **Kew Herbarium** *(open to specialists)* and a row of one-time royal "cottages," which include at no. 37 Cambridge Cottage, now home to the **Wood Museum** and **Kew Gardens Gallery** *(enter from inside the gardens).*

Musical Museum – *399 High St, Brentford. 020 8560 8108. www. musicalmuseum.co.uk. Open Fri–Sun 11am–5pm.* The museum's collection of some 200 mechanical music-makers—pianolas, organs, a Wurlitzer—is displayed in modern, brightly painted premises.

National Archives – *Ruskin Ave. 020 8876 3444. www.national archives.gov.uk. Open Wed, Fri , Sat 9am–5pm, Tue & Thu 9am–7pm.* The Domesday Book, Shakespeare's will, Guy Fawkes's confessions, and Captain Cook's charts are just a few of the precious historic documents entrusted to the PRO, founded in 1838 and formerly housed in Chancery Lane. Fragile papers are kept in controlled conditions but there are regular exhibitions of fascinating documents.

St Anne's Church – Largely constructed on the site of a 16C chapel in 1710–14, the royal gallery was added by George III in 1805. Gainsborough (d. 1788) is buried in the churchyard.

MUST SEE

CHISWICK★★

⊖Hammersmith; Turnham Green and Bus no. 190, or overground rail to Chiswick from Waterloo.
This delightful leafy suburb has a pretty riverside walk to Hammersmith Bridge past delightful pubs affording fine views of the river, where keen rowers are out in all weather. This is at the center of the annual Oxford and Cambridge **Boat Race** course *(see Fulham and Putney p 105).* In October, the 🚣 **Great River Race** *(www.greatriverrace. co.uk)* is a less serious affair, with up to 150 craft from Celtic curricles to Chinese dragon boats taking to the water from Richmond to London Docklands. Chiswick also boasts many elegant houses, including **Chiswick Mall★★**, with bow windows and balconies that overlook the river, the fine **St Nicholas** parish church *(www. stnicholaschiswick.org),* and many artistic and historic associations.

Chiswick House★ – *Burlington La. 020 8995 0508. www.chgt.org.uk. House: Open Apr daily 10am–5pm; May–Oct Sun–Wed & public holidays 10am–5pm. Gardens: Open daily year round 7am–dusk. House: £6.10.*

Classical symmetry at the heart of Chiswick House

© Chiswick House

A graceful neo-Palladian villa set in beautiful landscaped gardens and filled with fine furnishings and fabulous works of art.

Hogarth's House★ – *Hogarth La. 020 8994 6757. www.hounslow. info/arts/hogarthshouse. Tue–Sun noon–5pm.* Country home of the great painter and satirist from 1749 until his death in 1764; the walled garden still boasts his mulberry tree.

HAMPSTEAD★★ AND HIGHGATE

⊖Hampstead; Highgate.
High up on a hill lies the picturesque village of Hampstead, a maze of alleyways and passages, smart shops, and a lively café society in its bars and restaurants. Hampstead's glory lies in the rolling woodland and meadows of **Hampstead Heath** *(see Parks and Gardens),* enjoyed by walkers and film crews alike. Concerts and fairs are seasonal features. Highgate is also full of character, with some fine houses and pubs.

Hampstead village – The village, irregularly built on the side of a hill, has kept its original network of lanes, groves, alleyways, steps, courts, and rises. Home to affluent residents, this pleasant area has always attracted writers, artists, architects, and musicians. Don't miss **Flask Walk** (John Constable lived at no. 40), **Church Row, Frognal** (Kate Greenaway's house was no. 39), **Holly Walk, Admiral's Walk** (John Galsworthy lived at Grove Lodge), and **Vale of Heath**, a cluster of old cottages in a maze of narrow streets and paths.

EXCURSIONS

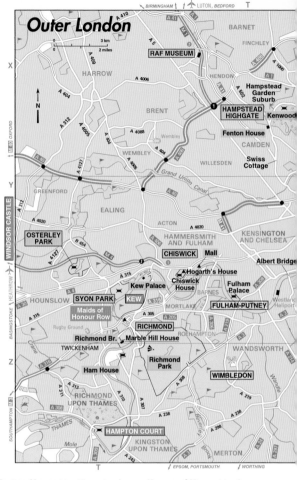

Outer London

Map labels:
BIRMINGHAM · LUTON, BEDFORD
BARNET
FINCHLEY
RAF MUSEUM
HARROW
HENDON
Hampstead Garden Suburb
HAMPSTEAD HIGHGATE
Kenwood
Fenton House
BRENT
CAMDEN
Wembley
WEMBLEY
Swiss Cottage
WILLESDEN
Grand Union Canal
GREENFORD
OXFORD
EALING
ACTON
KENSINGTON AND CHELSEA
OSTERLEY PARK
WINDSOR CASTLE
HAMMERSMITH AND FULHAM
CHISWICK
Mall
Albert Bridge
Hogarth's House
Chiswick House
Fulham Palace
Kew Palace
KEW
FULHAM-PUTNEY
Westland Heliport
SYON PARK
Maids of Honour Row
BARNES
MORTLAKE
HOUNSLOW
BASINGSTOKE / HEATHROW
Rugby Ground
RICHMOND
ROEHAMPTON
Richmond Br.
Marble Hill House
Crane
TWICKENHAM
Richmond Park
WANDSWORTH
Ham House
WIMBLEDON
SOUTHAMPTON
RICHMOND UPON THAMES
THAMES
Mole
HAMPTON COURT
KINGSTON UPON THAMES
MERTON
EPSOM, PORTSMOUTH
WORTHING

Scale: 3 km / 2 miles

Fenton House★★ – Hampstead Grove, Hampstead. 020 7435 3471. www.nationaltrust.org.uk/fentonhouse. Open Wed–Sun 11am–5pm. This red-brick house, built in 1693, is Hampstead's finest. The fine furniture and pictures form a background to 18C porcelain and a collection of early keyboards.

Kenwood House★★ – Bus no. 210 from Golders Green or Archway. Hampstead La, Hampstead. 0870 333 1181. www.english-heritage.org.uk. House: Open daily 10am–5pm. Grounds: Open daily 8am–dusk. Enlarged and embellished by Robert Adam in the 17C, Kenwood was purchased in 1925 by Lord Iveagh, who filled it with a remarkable collection

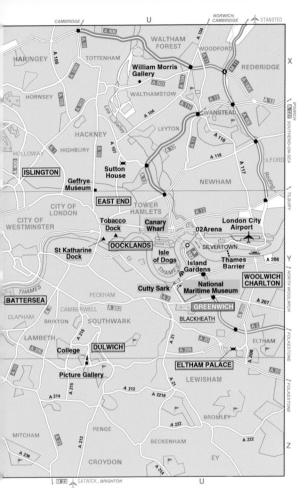

NORWICH, CAMBRIDGE
STANSTED

WALTHAM FOREST

WOODFORD

HARINGEY

TOTTENHAM

REDBRIDGE

William Morris Gallery

WALTHAMSTOW

HORNSEY

WANSTEAD

IPSWICH

SOUTHEND-ON-SEA

HACKNEY

LEYTON

ILFORD

HOLLOWAY

HIGHBURY

ISLINGTON

Sutton House

Geffrye Museum

NEWHAM

CITY OF LONDON

EAST END

CITY OF WESTMINSTER

TOWER HAMLETS

TILBURY

Tobacco Dock

Canary Wharf

O2 Arena

London City Airport

St Katharine Dock

DOCKLANDS

SILVERTOWN

Thames Barrier

Isle of Dogs

Island Gardens

THAMES

WOOLWICH CHARLTON

NORTH WOOLWICH

BATTERSEA

Cutty Sark

National Maritime Museum

GREENWICH

PECKHAM

CAMBERWELL

BLACKHEATH

CLAPHAM

BRIXTON

SOUTHWARK

LAMBETH

College

DULWICH

ELTHAM

FOLKESTONE

Picture Gallery

ELTHAM PALACE

LEWISHAM

MITCHAM

PENGE

FOLKESTONE

BROMLEY

BECKENHAM

CROYDON

EY

M23 GATWICK, BRIGHTON

of **paintings★★**. These include works by Rembrandt, Frans Hals, Vermeer, Va de Velde, Rubens, Gainsborough, Romney, and Reynolds. The beautiful **Adam Library★★** is richly decorated with Adam motifs and painted blue and old rose. The stunning landscaped parkland plays host to the summer season of **Picnic Concerts** *(see Live Music)*.

Burgh House – *New End Sq, Hampstead. 020 7431 0144. www. burghhouse.org.uk. House and Museum: Open Wed, Fri & Sun noon–5pm, Sat noon–5pm Art Gallery only.* This dignified, Grade I listed house, with its south-facing terrace, was built in 1703. The paneled rooms are now used for poetry and music recitals, exhibitions by local artists, and the **Hampstead Museum**.

Keats House, Hampstead

K. Brett/MICHELIN

Keats House – *Keats Grove, Hampstead. 020 7435 2062. www.cityoflondon.gov.uk. Open Tue–Sun 1–5pm (Nov–Apr Fri–Sun only).* Keats lodged here from 1818–20, and it was the setting that inspired some of his best-loved poems. The garden is free and is a popular picnicking spot.

2 Willow Road – *020 7435 6166. www.nationaltrust.org.uk. Open mid-Mar–Oct Thu–Sun 5pm. Entry by guided tour only 11am, noon, 1pm, and 2pm, unguided visits 3–5pm.* Designed by architect Ernö Goldfinger in 1939, this unique Modernist home has many elements considered groundbreaking at the time. The house contains the Goldfingers' impressive collection of modern art and innovative furniture.

Hampstead Residents, Old and New

In the cemetery lie Kate Greenaway, illustrator of children's books, and Laszlo Biro, inventor of the ballpoint pen. Residents have included John Constable, John Keats, Ian Fleming, Agatha Christie, Sting, Boy George, Elizabeth Taylor, Rex Harrison, Peter O'Toole, Emma Thompson, and Johnny Depp.

Highgate village – Highgate remains a village in character, centered on pretty **Pond Square** and the **High Street**. **The Grove**, a wide, tree-planted road has late 17C–early 18C rose-brick terrace houses (Coleridge lived at no. 3). **Bacon's Lane** honors philosopher Francis Bacon, who was a frequent guest (and died) at Arundel House, where **Old Hall** now stands.

Highgate Cemetery★★ – *Swains La. 020 8340 1834. www.highgatecemetery.org. East Cemetery open Mon–Fri 10am–4.30pm, Sat–Sun 11am–4.30pm. £4. West Cemetery by guided tour only, Mon–Fri 1.45pm, booked in advance only, Sat–Sun 11am–4pm half hourly, no bookings taken. £12.* Highgate Cemetery offers one of the most fascinating days out in London. Famous "residents" include George Eliot (d. 1880), Karl Marx (d. 1883), Michael Faraday (d. 1867), and Dante Gabriel and Christina Rossetti.

OSTERLEY PARK★★

⊖ *Osterley. 020 8232 5050. www.nationaltrust.org.uk. House: Open Mar–Oct Wed–Sun 11am–5pm. Gardens: Open daily 11am–5pm.*
Osterley Park is the place to see a Robert Adam interior at its most complete. Room after room is as he designed it: ceilings, walls, doors, handles, carpets, mirrors, and furniture. The rooms are elegantly furnished and decorated to reflect the tastes of wealthy and discerning owners. Outside, the **Pleasure Grounds** have been restored according to old maps and prints, with a Doric temple and

Adam's garden house (c 1780). The grounds, which include a chain of lakes, burst into fragrant, colorful blooms in summer.

RICHMOND★★

⊖ *Richmond; also accessible by boat from Westminster Pier.*

In an attractive riverside location, the vibrant town of Richmond has a rural atmosphere, with leafy parks, woodland, and golf courses. Together with neighboring **Twickenham** (the home of English rugby), Richmond is a highly desirable area. Fine mansions recall past aristocratic associations when Richmond Palace was a favorite residence of Tudor monarchs.

Once the scene of Tudor jousting, **Richmond Green** is surrounded with historic houses, including **Maids of Honour Row★★★, Trumpeters' House★**, and the **Gatehouse** from Richmond Palace. **Richmond Theatre**, which overlooks the Little Green, has been restored to its late 19C glory. A walk along the river reveals **Richmond Bridge★★**, built in 1774 and widened in 1937; tolls were levied until the 19C. **Asgill House★**, at the end of the lane overlooking the river, was built c. 1760.

The Old Town Hall houses the **Museum of Richmond** (*Whittaker Ave; 020 8332 1141; www.museum of richmond.com; open Tue–Sat 11am–5pm*). The **view★★** gets ever better as you climb **Richmond Hill**, lined with terraces immortalized by such artists as Turner and Reynolds. At the top, the gates to **Richmond Park★★** (*see Parks and Gardens*) are dated 1700 and attributed to "Capability" Brown.

Richmond Theatre

Pawel Libera/VisitLondon

Twickenham – *Rail: Twickenham; St Margaret's from Waterloo.* Nowadays Twickenham draws visitors to its rugby matches, rather than its sights (*see Sports London*), but the land adjacent to the river is occupied by many formal gardens, great pubs, and historic houses, including **York House**, **Bushy House**, and **Morgan House**.

Ham House★★ – *Rail: Twickenham from Waterloo. Ham St, Richmond-upon-Thames, TW10 7RS. 020 8940 1950. www.nationaltrust.org.uk. Open mid-Mar–Oct Sat–Thu noon–4pm. £11.* This unusually complete example of 17C opulence and wealth was at its prime under Elizabeth Dysart, Duchess of Lauderdale, member of the Sealed Knot, a secret royalist organization during the English Civil War.

Marble Hill House★ – *Across the river from Ham House (foot ferry). 0870 333 1181. www.english-heritage. org.uk. Open Apr–Nov Sat 10am–1.30pm, Sun 10.30am–5pm. £5.90.* The last of the Palladian mansions that once lined this stretch of the Thames, Marble Hill House was built in 1729 for Henrietta Howard, mistress of King George II.

ROYAL AIR FORCE MUSEUM★★

⊖Colindale *(10 min walk or bus no. 303 from station). Grahame Park Way, Hendon, NW9 5LL. 020 8205 2266. www.rafmuseum. org.uk. Open daily 10am–6pm (last admission 5.30pm). No charge.*
Magnificent flying machines and simulators inform and entertain at this well-presented museum with more than 200 aircraft as well as many smaller exhibits and interactive activities. The museum is housed in several hangars on the site of Old Hendon Airfield, where Grahame White established his flying school before World War I.

SYON PARK★★

Rail: Syon Lane, from Waterloo. 020 8560 0882. syonpark.info. Gardens: Open mid-Mar–Oct daily 10.30am–5.30pm. Open mid-Mar–Nov Wed, Thu, Sun, and public holidays 11am–5pm. House & gardens £11.50, gardens only £6.50.
The prospect of this splendid house, set in a vast park by the Thames and opposite Kew Gardens, is enchanting. Originally a Tudor mansion, **Syon House** has been the seat of an aristocratic family since the 16C. It contains some of Robert Adam's finest interiors, which were commissioned by the first Duke of Northumberland in the 18C.

Gardens★ – Designed by Capability Brown, the gardens boast a vast fragrant **rose garden** and the **Great Conservatory**, a beautiful semicircular building with a central cupola.

DULWICH★

Rail: West Dulwich from Victoria, North Dulwich from London Bridge.
The highlights of Dulwich are its pretty village, handsome weather-boarded buildings, elegant houses, and fine museums, including the **Horniman Museum★★★** *(see For Kids).* The area is also home to a vast park with magnificent oak trees and a large lake. **Dulwich College★** *(College Rd)* was founded by Edward Alleyn, one of the greatest actors of the late 16C, as a school for poor children. The original buildings include the chapel where Alleyn is buried. **Dulwich College**, one of Britain's top Independent boys' schools, is farther down the road. Opened in 1814, **Dulwich Picture Gallery★** *(Gallery Rd; 020 8693 5254; www. dulwichpicturegallery.org.uk),* is the oldest public gallery in the country. It includes works by Rembrandt, Gainsborough, Reynolds, Van Dyck, Raphael, Tiepolo, Canaletto, Rubens, and Murillo.

FULHAM AND PUTNEY

⊖Putney Bridge.
These fine residential areas linked by a bridge enjoy a pleasant riverside location. Fulham has become an offshoot of fashionable Chelsea, while Putney, with its leafy

Great Conservatory, Syon Park

K. Brett/MICHELIN

Oxford and Cambridge Boat Race, Putney

K. Brett/MICHELIN

common, has a rural atmosphere.
All Saints Church in Fulham
(Church Gate; 020 7736 3264) and
St Mary's Church in Putney
*(at the approach to Putney bridge;
020 8788 4414)* are both worth
a visit.

Fulham Palace – *Bishop's Ave. 020
7736 8140. www.fulhampalace.org.
Grounds: Open daily dawn–dusk.
Museum: Open Wed–Sat 1–4pm.*
The palace, which retains the
appearance of a modest Tudor
manor, was the official summer
residence of the Bishop of London
from 704 to 1973. *The **museum**
traces the history of the site, the
buildings, and the gardens.* The
attractive gardens include the first
magnolia to be grown in Britain,
exotic species, a fragrant herb
garden, and a pretty **wisteria walk**.

Putney Bridge – The bridge
marks the beginning of the
Oxford and Cambridge **Boat Race**
(4.5mi/7km to Mortlake), a hotly
contested rowing race between
Oxford and Cambridge
Universities that began in 1829.

WIMBLEDON
⊖ *Wimbledon; Southfields;
Wimbledon Park.*

In addition to its thriving village
perched on a hilltop, vast common
land, a windmill, and a golf course,
Wimbledon takes great pride in its
acclaimed **Tennis Championship**
(see Sports London), which draws
international stars every summer.
St Mary's Church *(Church Rd; 020
8946 2605)* was mentioned in the
Domesday Book.

Wimbledon Common – The horse
racing, dueling, and drilling of
soldiers of earlier days have now
given way to horse riding, cricket,
rugby, and golf. The 18C saw
several large mansions rise around
the Common: **King's College
School** (1750), **Southside House**
(1776) *(Woodhayes Rd; 020 8946
7643; guided tours),* **Chester House**
(1670), and **Cannizaro** (1727,
rebuilt in 1900) *(Cannizaro Park
open daily).*

Museums – **Wimbledon
Museum** *(Ridgway; 020 8296 9914;
www.wimbledonmuseum.org.uk),*
housed in the Village Club, focuses
on local history. **Wimbledon
Windmill Museum** *(Windmill Rd;
020 8947 2825; www.wimbledon
windmill.org.uk), located in a
converted hollow post mill,*
illustrates the story of windmills.

FOR KIDS

You'll be spoilt for choice finding things to keep the little ones amused in the city. Children's playgrounds in most parks are popular and there are plenty of activities for children of all ages. Museums and galleries have special programs, from treasure hunts to storytelling and even sleepovers to engage children's imagination. Visit London have a special section on their website (www.visitlondon.com) for families; *Time Out* magazine *(www.timeout.com)* carries special children's supplements during half-term and the school vacations.

MUSEUMS

The wonderful exhibits of the **Natural History Museum**★★ *(see p 82)* bring ecological and environmental issues to the fore; the Dinosaur and Creepy Crawlies exhibits are ever popular. Children take part in experiments relating to scientific and technological advances, which are entertainingly presented at the **Science Museum**★★★ *(see p 80)*. The mummies at the **British Museum**★★★ *(see p 78)* are particular favorites. Exciting maritime adventures are told at the **National Maritime Museum**★★★ *(see p 79)*. Both the **V&A** *(see p 81)* and the **Imperial War Museum**★★★ *(see p 79)* stage special events and exhibitions aimed at children, while the **Cartoon Museum** *(see p 68)* is always a winner.

Horniman Museum★★★

Rail: Forest Hill from London Bridge. 100 London Rd, SE23 3PQ. 020 8699 1872. www.horniman.ac.uk. Museum: Open daily 10.30am–5.30pm. Gardens: Mon–Sat 7.15am–sunset, Sun and public holidays 8am–sunset. No charge. Off map. Possibly the best of the lot, the Horniman has a wonderful array of children's activities, many based around its superb collection of some 7,000 **musical instruments** from around the world. The museum was founded in 1901 when Frederick Horniman, a Victorian tea trader, left his house and collections of curiosities to the people of London. Now much expanded, it is one of the most original in London, and winner of numerous awards. The exhibits in the **African Worlds and Centenary**

Central Hall, Natural History Museum

©Natural History Museum

MUST DO

Galleries include African masks, Navajo textiles, and carvings of Asian gods. The **European** collection concentrates on folk art. The **Pacific** area includes material from Polynesia. The **gardens**, with formal rose gardens and a children's petting zoo, host outdoor concerts in summer.

London Transport Museum ★

⊖ Covent Garden. 39 Wellington St, WC2E 7BB. 020 7565 7299 (info). www.ltmuseum.co.uk. Open daily 10am–6pm (Fri 11am). Adults £15, children 17 and under free.

This museum, housed in part of the old flower market, shows the development of one of the world's earliest and largest transport networks from trams and trolleybuses to the driverless trains used by the Docklands Light Railway. Throughout the museum there are interactive activities and real vehicles, including London's beloved Routemaster bus, finally taken out of service in 2005. (The **Routemaster** still runs along two heritage routes: the no. 9 from the Royal Albert Hall to Aldwych, and the no. 15, which passes Tower Bridge, Oxford St, and Trafalgar Sq.)

Museum of Childhood at Bethnal Green

⊖ Bethnal Green. Cambridge Heath Rd, E2 9PA. 020 8983 5200. www.vam.ac.uk/moc. Open daily 10am–5.45pm. No charge.

The museum houses the V&A's enchanting collection of toys, dolls, games, and puppets, as well as children's clothing, furniture, paintings, books, and other artifacts of childhood. The building, an iron and glass construction,

Type B Bus, London Transport Museum

London Transport Museum

was originally erected for the 1851 Great Exhibition; it was moved to the present site and opened in 1872.

Pollock's Toy Museum and Shop

⊖ Goodge St. 1 Scala St, W1T 2HL. 020 7636 3452. www.pollock stoymuseum.com. Open Mon–Sat 10am–5pm. Closed public holidays. Adults £5, children £2.

This wonderfully eccentric and enchanting museum takes its name from Benjamin Pollock, the last of the Victorian toy theater printers. Here, toys of yesteryear are displayed in an atmospheric setting of small rooms, connected by narrow winding staircases. The collection of 19C and 20C toys includes toy theaters, dolls, teddy bears, mechanical toys, carved wooden animals, dolls' houses, puppets, and board games. Live toy theater performances are staged during the school vacations and there's a toy shop proper on the ground floor.

FOR KIDS

107

HISTORIC LONDON

London is steeped in history, but it certainly isn't all dull and boring. There's plenty of pageantry, as well as exciting places and ghoulish tales that will capture the imagination of the most hard-to-please child. The **Whispering Gallery★★** in St Paul's *(see p 40)* holds a fascination for children. The **Tower of London★★★** *(see p 73)*, with its grim history, wealth of armor, ravens, and sparkling jewels will keep them amused for hours. For junior pirates there are ships to visit along the Thames and the colorful **Horse Guards★★★**, **Changing of the Guard Ceremony★★★**, and **Guards Museum** *(see p 75)* will keep many a young visitor happy.

Changing of the Guard★★★

⊖*Green Park. Buckingham Palace forecourt. On fair days May–Jul daily 11.30am, on alternate days rest of year.*

The ceremony takes place on the forecourt of **Buckingham Palace★★** *(see p 75)* when the Queen is in residence and the Royal

Colorful pageantry of the foot guards

Lee Frost / age fotostock

Royal Armor

The **Royal Armouries Collection** at the Tower of London *(see p 73)* contains Henry VIII's suit of armor made in 1520, when the king was 29; it weighed 49lb/22kg. A larger suit was made in 1540 for both the king and his horse. There is also a small gilt suit with helmet, thought to be made for Charles I as a boy (c 1610).

Standard is flying. The guard is mounted by the five regiments of Foot of the Guards Division in their uniform of scarlet tunics and lofty bearskins.

Horse Guards★★★

⊖*Charing Cross; Westminster. 020 7414 2353. www.army.mod.uk. Ceremonial mounting of the Queen's Life Guard★★★ daily 11am (Sun 10am) in Horse Guards Parade; dismount ceremony daily 4pm in the Front Yard of Horse Guards.*

This plain building acts as the official entrance to Buckingham Palace and as such is where all dignitaries on official visits are greeted. It is guarded by mounted sentries, alternating between the Life Guards in scarlet tunics and white plumed helmets, and the Blues and Royals in blue with red plumes.

Cutty Sark★★

⊖*North Greenwich. 020 8858 2698. www.cuttysark.org.uk. Open daily 10am–5pm. £13.50 (children £7). See map p 101.*

Launched in 1869 for the China tea trade, the Cutty Sark was the fastest clipper in the world in her heyday. In 1922 she was converted into a nautical training school and

MUST DO

transferred to dry dock at Greenwich in 1954. In May 2007 Cutty Sark was badly damaged by fire. The conservation process placed the ship in a dry dock, allowing visitors to walk beneath the awe-inspiring hull, while an onboard exhibition explores the ship's history and contemporary society.

HMS Belfast
⊖ *London Bridge. Tooley St, SE1 2JH. 020 7940 6300. www.hms belfast.iwm.org.uk. Open Mar–Oct daily 10am–6pm; Nov–Feb daily 10am–5pm. Adults £15.50, children under 16 free.*
One of the most powerful large light cruisers ever built, *HMS Belfast* is the only surviving vessel of her type to have seen active service during World War II, including work with the Arctic convoys and on D-Day. Painted in the original camouflage colors and bristling with 12 6in/30cm guns, seven decks are on display. Saved from destruction in 1971, *HMS Belfast* is the first ship to be preserved for the nation since Nelson's *Victory*.

The Golden Hinde
⊖ *London Bridge. St Mary Overie Dock, Clink St, SE1 9DG. 020 7403 0123. Open daily 10am–5.30pm. Adult £6, child £4.50. .*
Sample a taste of Tudor life and experience the spartan conditions on board in a full-sized replica of the Tudor warship in which Sir Francis Drake circumnavigated the globe in 1577–80. There are also special events such as **Pirate Fun Days** and **Family Overnight Tours**.

Tower Bridge Exhibition
⊖ *Tower Hill; London Bridge, 202–3 Grange Rd, SE1 3AA. 020 7403*

HMS Belfast

©HMS Belfast/Imperial War Museum

3761. www.towerbridge.org.uk. Open Apr–Sept 10am–6pm; Oct–Mar 9.30am–5.30pm. Adults £9, children 5–15 £3.90, under-5s free.
Step inside the most famous bridge in the world *(see p 65)*, learn about its construction and history, then visit the Victorian Engine Rooms. Special events for kids take place in the high-level walkways during school vacations, including Victorian games and film shows.

THE NATURAL WORLD
The London parks are full of wild- life, from the almost-tame deer in **Richmond Park★★** to the pelicans in **St James's Park★★** *(see p 93)*; don't miss the petting zoo at **Battersea Park** *(see p 94)*. For a broader experience, visit **London Zoo★★**, where you can watch the antics of the inmates and adopt an animal. The **London Aquarium★** is home to one of Europe's largest collections of marine life. The planetarium at the **Royal Observatory Greenwich★★** *(see p 63)* has exciting presentations of the heavens.

FOR KIDS

109

London Zoo★★

⊖ *Camden Town. Regent's Park, NW14RY. 020 7722 3333. www.zsl. org/zsl-london-zoo. Open daily from 10am, closing time varies according to season (generally 6pm). Adults £26 (£24 online), children £18.50 (£17.50 online), under-3s free.*

In 1828 the Zoological Society of London opened a small menagerie in Regent's Park. Today the zoo has almost 750 different species and its objective is to conserve and breed endangered species and rare animals. Highlights include:

- **Animal Adventure**, the revamped children's zoo.
- **Aquarium**.
- **Blackburn Bird Pavilion**.
- The **B.U.G.S** exhibit.
- **Butterfly Paradise**.
- **Clore Rainforest Lookout**.
- **Gorilla Kingdom**.
- **Lion Terraces**.

We're all going to the zoo...

The zoo's program of daily events includes animal feeding times, bath time for the elephants, animals in the Amphitheater, and animal encounters in which the keepers introduce the animals in their charge.

Regal tiger at London Zoo

©Zoological Society of London

- The **Meerkats**.
- The **Meet the Monkeys** area.
- **Reptile House**.

London Aquarium★

⊖ *Charing Cross. County Hall, Westminster Bridge Rd, SE1 7PB. 0871 663 1678. www.sealife.co.uk/ london. Open daily 10am–7pm. Adults £21.60 (from £18.36 online), children 3–15 £15.90 (from £13.52 online), under-3s free.*

A monumental aquarium in the basement of **County Hall★** *(see p 56)* and reaching two floors below the Thames water level. Highlights include moon jellyfish and friendly rays, which come up to be tickled. Opposite the Aquarium, on the north bank is **Westminster Pier**, from which boat trips run frequently down river to the **Thames Barrier** *(www. westminsterpier.co.uk)*. The futuristic barrier protects central London from surge tides.

FUN AND GAMES

A trip on the **London Eye★** is an absolute must. The grisly exhibits of the **London Dungeon** and the Chamber of Horrors at **Madame Tussauds★** will bring thrills and chills. For creative types, the activities at the **Tate Britain★★★** *(see p 85)* and brass rubbing in the crypt of **St Martin-in-the-Fields★** *(see p 34)* should satisfy their talents. When they tire of museums and need some fresh air, London parks offer a wealth of activities. The adventure playground in **Holland Park** *(see p 95)* is recommended, as are the playground and paddling pool at **Hyde Park Lido** *(see p 92)* and the ice rink at **Somerset House★★** *(see p 31)* in winter.

MUST DO

🎡 London Eye★

⊖ *Waterloo. Southbank. 0870 5000 600. www.londoneye.com. Open daily Oct–Mar 10am–8pm; Apr–Sept 10am–9pm (Jul–Aug 9.30pm). Adults and children 4–15£29.50 (£26.55 online), under 4s free. Advance booking recommended.*

The giant wheel, a spectacular addition to London's skyline and one of its most popular tourist attractions, is the largest observation wheel ever built. Accommodated in closed pods, sightseers enjoy unparalleled **views★★★** across the city *(trip 30min).*

Madame Tussauds★

⊖ *Baker St. Marylebone Rd, NW1 5LR. 0870 400 3000. www.madametussauds.com. Open Mon–Fri 9.30am–5.30pm, Sat–Sun 9am–6pm. Adult £30 (£22.50 0nline), child £25.80 (£19.29 online).Advance booking recommended.*

Marie Grosholtz honed her wax modeling skills making death masks of guillotine victims in the French Revolution. Figures are arranged by theme in regularly updated exhibitions. Visitors can mingle with famous personalities from the worlds of entertainment, sport, politics, science, art, and royalty. The Chamber of Horrors, which should be avoided by the young or faint-hearted, lines up a selection of ghoulish murderers and serial killers.

London Dungeon

⊖ *London Bridge. 34 Tooley St. 0871 360 2049. www.thedungeons. com. Open daily 9.30am–7pm (seasonal variations apply).*

Entrance to the London Dungeon
©The London Dungeon

Adult £25.20 (from £17.50 0nline), children (15 and under) £19.80 (from £15.95 online). Advance booking recommended.

A gruesome (if rather ham-horror) parade of tableaux relating scenes of death, medieval torture, and various types of execution. Not suitable for young children or anyone with a nervous disposition (the exhibits have a way of "coming alive"!).

London Brass Rubbing Centre

⊖ *Charing Cross. St Martin-in-the-Fields, Trafalgar Sq. 020 7766 1122. Open daily Mon–Sat 10am–6pm (Thu–Sat 8pm), Sun 11.30am–5pm.*

Located in the vaulted crypt of St Martin-in-the-Fields, the center has replicas of brasses from churches in all parts of the country and from abroad. Prices start at £4.50.

FOR KIDS

BOX OFFICE

STAGE AND SCREEN

At all times of the year London offers everything from serious theater to top blockbusting musicals and the latest movie releases. Experimental drama is found in the "fringe" theaters. During the summer, venues in Holland Park, Regent's Park, and the Globe Theatre offer open-air performances (weather permitting!). Most of the mid-range theaters are located in the West End in and around Shaftesbury Avenue in Soho, near a wide range of restaurants offering pre- and post-theater set meals.

Theaters

The theaters listed here are some of the better known that feature long-running plays and musicals. For a complete list of current shows, consult the listings magazines or free London newspapers. Tickets for West End theaters booked by agents carry a surcharge. To avoid this buy seats directly from the theater box office. Matinées are cheaper, although star casts may be replaced by understudies.

Adelphi

⊖ *Charing Cross. Strand, WC2E 7NA. 0844 412 4651.*
Several Dickens' novels were adapted for the stage here soon after publication (1837–45). The theater is noted for some great musical productions (*Me and My Girl*, *Sunset Boulevard*, and *Chicago*).

Apollo Victoria Theatre

⊖ *Victoria. 17 Wilton Rd, Victoria, SW1V 1LG. 0844 826 8000. www.apollovictorialondon.org.uk.*
Recent productions at this former cinema (built 1930) include *Starlight Express* and *Wicked*.

Barbican Arts Centre

⊖ *Barbican. Barbican Centre, Silk St, EC2Y 8DS. 020 7638 8891. www.barbican.org.uk. Box office: Open Mon–Sat 9am–8pm, Sun 11am–8pm.*
Located in the **Barbican★**, a concrete neighborhood project conceived in the aftermath of World War II, the arts complex (1982) houses a concert hall, gallery, three cinemas, exhibition areas, and restaurants. The two theaters offer a range of productions from experimental cabaret to dance, classical theater, and new plays.

Dominion

⊖ *Tottenham Court Rd. 268–269 Tottenham Court Rd, W1T 0AG. 020 7580 1889. www.dominion theatre.co.uk.*
Built as a concert hall in a former leprosarium and brewery, and formerly a cinema, the Dominion is now famous for its musicals such as *Grease* and *We Will Rock You*.

Duke of York's Theatre

⊖ *Leicester Sq. St Martin's La, WC2N 4BG. 0870 060 6623.*
Its name is synonymous with playwrights such as Shaw, Ibsen, Galsworthy, and Noel Coward.

Her Majesty's Theatre

⊖ *Piccadilly Circus. Haymarket, St James's, SW1Y 4QL. 0844 412 4648. www.rutheatres.com.*
Designed in 1896, this Victorian theater seats 1,200. The musical the *Phantom of the Opera* has been running here since 1986.

MUST DO

🎫 Tkts (Half-Price Ticket Booth)

Run by the Society of London Theatres (SOLT) and based at Leicester Square, tkts offers a limited number of half-price tickets to most West End shows on the day of performance. Available on a first come, first served basis, only cash/credit/debit payment accepted (plus service charge), no returns. Visitors can also book full-price advance tickets for shows here. *Open Mon–Sat 10am–7pm, Sun 11am–4pm. For information, contact SOLT, 32 Rose St, WC2E 9ET. 020 7557 6700. www.tkts.co.uk.*

London Palladium
⊖ *Oxford Circus. 8 Argyll St, Soho, W1F 7TF. 0844 412 4648.*
Now more than 100 years old, this sumptuous theater is famous for staging lavish variety shows and spectacular major musicals.

Lyceum
⊖ *Covent Garden. 21 Wellington St, Covent Garden, WC2E 7RQ. 020 7420 8100. www.lyceumtheatre london.org.uk.*
The fourth theater to be built on this site, the Lyceum was once noted for ballets and classical plays. Today the theater stages mega-musicals such as *The Lion King*.

The Old Vic
⊖ *Waterloo. 103 The Cut, Lambeth, SE1 8NB. 0844 871 7628. www.oldvictheatre.com. Pit Bar: Open from 6pm (Sat 1pm).*
Former home of the National Theatre, the Old Vic opened in 1818 as the Coburg Theatre. Now under the artistic leadership of Kevin Spacey, it offers a range of theater, including a Christmas pantomime.

🎫 Open Air Theatre
⊖ *Baker St. Inner Circle, Regent's Park, NW1 4NR. 0844 826 4242. Box office: Open Mon–Sun 9am–9pm. www.openairtheatre.org. Performances May–Sept.*

In summer the New Shakespeare Company, founded in 1932, stages productions here, including such favorites as *A Midsummer Night's Dream*. Bring warm clothing, a cushion, an umbrella, and a picnic. Barbecue and cold buffet available.

Palace Theatre
⊖ *Leicester Sq. Shaftesbury Ave, Soho, W1D 8AY. 0844 412 4648. www.rutheatres.com.*
Opened as an opera house by Richard D'Oyly Carte, this grandiose building retains its Victorian atmosphere. It is now a venue for large-scale musicals.

Queen's Theatre
⊖ *Piccadilly Circus. Shaftesbury Ave, W1V 8BA. 0844 482 5160.*
Partially rebuilt after bomb damage in World War II and now owned by Sir Cameron Mackintosh's company, Queen's has been refurbished and modernised and remains home to long-running musical *Les Miserables*.

Royal Court Theatre
⊖ *Sloane Sq. Sloane Sq, SW1W 8AS. 020 7565 5000. www.royalcourttheatre.com.*
This theater has assumed a pioneering role since 1956 when the English Stage Co under

Royal Court Theatre

George Devine presented John Osborne's *Look Back in Anger*.

Royal National Theatre★★
⊖ *Waterloo. South Bank, SE1 9PX. 020 7452 3000. www.nationaltheatre.org.uk. Box office: Open Mon–Sat 9.30am–8pm. Guided tours.*
The National Theatre Company, founded by Sir Laurence Olivier in 1962, has been based in this modern building since 1976, with three theaters: the **Olivier**, the **Lyttelton**, and the **Cottesloe**.

Shakespeare's Globe★★
⊖ *Blackfriars; Cannon St; London Bridge; Southwark; Waterloo. 21 New Globe Walk, Bankside, SE1 9DT. 020 7401 9919. www.shakespearesglobe.com. Theater season Apr–Oct. Box office: Open Mon–Sat 10am–6pm. Open daily for tours and exhibition 9am–5pm (Apr–Oct Globe afternoon tours Mon only), £13.50.*
Located on the south bank of the Thames, the Globe is identical to the original Elizabethan theater destroyed in 1644 by the order of the Church. A museum and theater, performances are held in the afternoons and evenings *(Apr–Oct)*. The audience sit on hard benches or stand in the pit. Alongside the main theater, the **Inigo Jones Theatre**, a small playhouse built according to Jones' drawings, stages concerts and productions all year round.

Theatre Royal Drury Lane
⊖ *Covent Garden. Drury Lane, WC2B 5JF. 0844 412 4648.*
The first theater on this site (1663) was patronized by Charles II who

Globe Theatre

met Nell Gwynne here. The second, designed by Wren, knew a golden age under Garrick (1747–76). The third theater (1794) opened with Sheridan's new play *The School for Scandal.* The present Georgian building, which saw the likes of Kean, Irving, and Ellen Terry, now hosts popular musicals.

Theatre Royal Haymarket★
⊖ Piccadilly Circus. 1 Haymarket, SW1Y 4HT. 0845 481 1870.
There has been a theater on this site since 1720, making it the third-oldest London playhouse still in use. The current elegant building was designed by Nash in 1821.

Cinemas

BFI London IMAX Cinema
⊖ Waterloo. 1 Charlie Chaplin Walk, South Bank, SE1 8XR. 0870 787 2525. www.bfi.org.uk.
This circular 500-seat cinema screens 2D and 3D films on an 85ft/26m-wide screen— the biggest in the UK.

BFI Southbank
⊖ Waterloo. Belvedere Rd, SE1 8XT. 020 7928 3232. www.bfi.org.uk.
The BFI Southbank comprises four cinemas and a studio offering a program of films from the BFI archive and new releases not shown elsewhere. It also hosts the annual Times BFI London Film Festival.

Odeon Cinemas
⊖ Leicester Sq. 22–24 Leicester Sq, Soho, WC2H 7LQ. 0871 224 4007. www.odeon.co.uk. Open daily 11am–9pm.

London's biggest cinema (1,943 seats), where the premieres of prestigious British and Hollywood films are shown.

Ritzy Picturehouse
⊖ Brixton. Brixton Oval, Coldharbour La, Brixton, SW2 1JG. 0871 902 5739. www.picturehouses.co.uk.
This Edwardian cinema shows both classics and recent films.

Comedy clubs

The Comedy Store
⊖ Piccadilly Circus; Leicester Sq. 1a Oxendon St, SW1Y 4EE. www.thecomedystore.co.uk.
Many famous and cutting-edge stand-up comedians have played here. The seating is not the most comfortable, but the atmosphere more than makes up for it.

HMV Hammersmith Apollo
⊖ Hammersmith. Queen Caroline St, Hammersmith, W6 9QH. 0844 844 4748.
Some of the best UK comedians take center stage here to packed audiences. The Apollo also hosts popular music concerts.

Auditorium, HMV Hammersmith Apollo

©HMV Apollo

STAGE AND SCREEN

LIVE MUSIC

London is one of the concert, opera, and pop capitals of the world. Opera is staged in venues such as the Royal Albert Hall and Covent Garden Piazza. Happy crowds enjoy the Last Night of the Proms in Hyde Park and the open-air concerts at Holland Park, Hampton Court, and Kenwood. Pop and rock stars are equally at home at the O2 Arena, Wembley Arena, and Docklands London Arena; the Royal Festival Hall and the Barbican host jazz, folk, and world music along with a superb array of classical concerts, while small clubs showcase a mix of new artists and old favorites.

🎵 Opera and ballet

Prices for opera and ballet vary enormously, but good tickets will be expensive. In summer, live opera and ballet are broadcast on giant screens in **Covent Garden Piazza** *(see City of Westminster)* to enthusiastic crowds *(inquire at box office or check online for dates)*. Tickets are free but cannot be booked in advance, so get there early.

English National Opera
⊖ *Leicester Sq; Charing Cross. London Coliseum, St Martin's La, WC2N 4ES. 0871 911 0200. www.eno.org. Box office open 24hr.*
This large theater, built in 1904 to rival Drury Lane, is spectacular, with marble pillars and a lavish interior. Since 1968 it's been home to the English National Opera.

Royal Opera House★
⊖ *Covent Garden. Bow St, WC2E 9DD. 020 7304 4000. www.roh.org.uk. Box office: Open Mon–Sat 10am–8pm.*
In 1999 after extensive renovation, one of the world's most prestigious opera houses reopened to reveal a new splendor. The iron-and-glass Floral Hall is used to great effect as the main foyer with escalators rising to the mezzanine galleries with panoramic views of the piazza. Tickets are expensive and can be difficult to obtain.

Classical elegance of the Opera House

Rob Moore/Royal Opera House

Sadler's Wells Theatre
⊖*Angel. Rosebery Ave, Islington, EC1R 4TN. 0844 412 4300. www. sadlerswells.com. Box office: Open Mon–Sat 9am–8.30pm.*
The only London theater to present classical ballet and contemporary dance.

Classical music
London offers a range of classical music performed by world-class artists. Prices vary but you can hear some first-class music for just a few pounds. **Westminster Abbey**, **Westminster Cathedral**, and **St Paul's Cathedral** all boast superb choirs that you can hear for free. City churches that organize lunchtime concerts include **St Bride's**, **St Anne and St Agnes**, **St Lawrence Jewry**, **St Margaret Lothbury**, **St Martin-within-Ludgate**, **St Mary-le-Bow**, and **St Michael's Cornhill**.

Barbican Hall
⊖*Barbican. Silk St, EC2Y 8DS. 020 7638 8891. www.barbican. org.uk. Box office: Open Mon–Sat 9am–8pm, Sun 11am–8pm.*
Home to the London Symphony Orchestra, the hall is also used by touring orchestras (see p 112).

Royal Festival Hall★
⊖*Waterloo. Belvedere Rd, South Bank, SE1 8XX. 0844 875 0073 (box office). www.southbankcentre. co.uk. Open daily 10am–11pm.*
The Royal Festival Hall, built in 1951 as part of the Festival of Britain, is the home of the London Philharmonic Orchestra. Programs range from large-scale orchestral concerts, ballet, films, and opera, to the London Jazz Festival.
The two smaller venues, **Queen Elizabeth Hall** and **Purcell Room**,

The Festival of Britain
In 1951 some 8.5 million people visited the Festival where they learned about British achievement in arts, sciences, and industrial design, and enjoyed the Pleasure Gardens in Battersea Park. The small site on the South Bank was dominated by the Skylon, a cigar-shaped vertical feature that appeared to float in midair, and the Dome of Discovery, a circular pavilion made of steel and aluminum.

host contemporary dance, music theater, chamber music, recitals, world music, poetry, and live art.

St James's Church Concerts
⊖*Piccadilly Circus. 197 Piccadilly, W1J 9LL. 020 7734 4511. www.sjp.org.uk.*
Lunchtime recitals (*Mon, Wed, Fri 1.10pm; suggested donation £3.50*) and evening classical concerts (*Thu–Sat 7.30pm*).

St John's, Smith Square
⊖*Westminster. Smith Sq, Westminster, SW1P 3HA. 020 7222 1061. www.sjss.org.uk. Box office: Open Mon–Fri 10am–5pm.*
This Grade I listed church is the setting for the annual Lufthansa Festival of baroque music. Lunchtime concerts (*Mon 1pm*) and evening chamber and vocal music events.

St Martin-in-the-Fields
⊖*Charing Cross. Trafalgar Sq, WC2N 4JJ. 020 7766 1100. www2. stmartin-in-the-fields.org.*
Tickets are available for evening concerts (*Tue–Sat 7.30pm*) by from

the Crypt box office (open Mon–Sat 10am–5pm, Thu–Sat 8.30pm).

Royal Albert Hall
⊖ South Kensington. Kensington Gore, SW7 2AP. 0845 401 5034. www.royalalberthall.com. Box office: Open daily 9am–9pm.
Home to "The Proms" (mid-Jul–mid-Sep), and to the Royal Philharmonic Orchestra, the Hall hosts a wide range of concerts and events.

Wigmore Hall
⊖ Bond St; Oxford Circus. 36 Wigmore St, Marylebone, W1U 2BP. 020 7935 2141. www.wigmore-hall.org.uk. Box office: Open daily 10am–8.30pm.
A lovely intimate hall, ideal for solo recitals and chamber orchestras. Sunday morning coffee-concerts.

Rock, roots, & jazz

Cecil Sharp House
⊖ Camden Town. 2 Regent's Park Rd, Camden, NW1 7AY. 020 7485 2206. www.efdss.org.
An arts venue hosting concerts of folk music, singing, and dancing.

Dover Street Restaurant & Bar
⊖ Green Park. 8–10 Dover St, W1S 4LQ. 020 7491 7509. www.doverst.co.uk.
Jazz bar-restaurant with live music and dancing nightly from 10.30pm. Dress smartly.

HMV Forum
⊖ Kentish Town. 9–17 Highgate Rd, Kentish Town, NW5 1JY. 0844 847 2405. www.kentishtown forum.com. Open daily 7–11pm (Fri–Sat 2am).
Opened in 1934 as a movie house, this Art Deco building has a

capacity for 2,000; big bands and rock stars love its intimate charm.

Jazz Café
⊖ Camden Town. 3–5 Parkway, Camden, NW1 7PG. 0870 060 3777. www.jazzcafe.co.uk. Open daily 7pm–2am.
Jazz, soul, Latin American, and African rap music every evening in this intimate club.

O2 Academy Brixton
⊖ Brixton. 211 Stockwell Rd, Brixton, SW9 9SL. 020 7771 3000. www.O2academybrixton.co.uk.
Immense hall with an Art Deco interior, considered by many to be London's best concert hall. Many greats started out here, including the Rolling Stones, David Bowie, Jamiroquai, and UB40.

Pizza Express Jazz Club
⊖ Tottenham Court Rd. 10 Dean St, Soho, W1D 3RW. 0845 602 7017. www.pizzaexpresslive.com. Open daily noon–midnight.
Excellent modern jazz in the basement room.

Ronnie Scott's
⊖ Leicester Sq. 47 Frith St, Soho, W1D 4HT. 020 7439 0747. www.ronniescotts.co.uk. Open Mon–Sat 6pm–3am, Sun 6pm–midnight; music from 7.30pm (book in advance).
Legendary Soho jazz club, with outstanding music and atmosphere.On Mondays to Thursdays, after the main act, Ronnie's opens itself up for **The Late Late Show**, when audiences can enjoy a classic late-night jazz "hang" that harks back to the club's early days (11pm until the small hours).

O2 Arena at the Millennium Dome

Riverside walks, green parkland, and lakes have transformed the Greenwich peninsula, but its focal point is the Dome, built to mark the third millennium. After years of wrangling over its fate, this controversial structure has been transformed into the **O2 Arena**, a concert venue, sports arena, and exhibition space.

⊖*North Greenwich. Peninsula Sq, SE10 0DX. 020 8463 2000. www.theo2.co.uk. Open 9am till late (last admission 1am). There is also a regular boat service from Waterloo Pier (www.thamesclippers.com).*

Ronnie Scott's

©Ronnie Scott's

Shepherd's Bush Empire

⊖*Shepherd's Bush. Shepherd's Bush Green, W12 8TT. 0844 477 2000, 020 8354 3300. www.o2 shepherdsbush empire.co.uk. Box office open show days 4pm.*
Built in the early 20C, "The Empire" bought by the BBC in 1953, played a major role in the history of television. Today it's a concert hall with excellent acoustics.

100 Club

⊖*Oxford Circus. 100 Oxford St, W1D 1LL. 020 7636 0933. www.the100club.co.uk. Check website for opening times.*
This basement venue, where the Sex Pistols made their debut, highlights traditional jazz, modern jazz, blues, and swing.

606 Club

⊖*Earl's Court. 90 Lots Rd, Chelsea, SW10 0QD. 020 7352 5953. www.606club.co.uk. Check website for opening times.*
Book a table for dinner to hear top British jazz musicians perform at this atmospheric basement venue.

🌿 Open-air venues

Open-air venues are growing ever more popular with Londoners. **Hyde Park** *(see p 92)*, **Holland Park** *(see p 95)*, and **Somerset House★★** *(see p 31)* all host summer concerts. The world-famous Last Night of the Proms is broadcast live to Hyde Park crowds in a real party mood. You can also hear live music at **Covent Garden Piazza★★** *(see p 36)*, **Victoria Embankment Gardens★** *(see p 94)*, and **Broadgate** *(see p 47)*. **Kenwood House** *(Rail: Gospel Oak/Hampstead Heath; Hampstead La, NW3 7JR; 020 8348 1286; www.picnicconcerts. com)* hosts its annual season of **Picnic Concerts**, held in in the breathtaking setting of its landscaped gardens and featuring classical music and big name artists.

LIVE MUSIC

NIGHTLIFE

London's energetic club scene is a major attraction. The city is filled with late-night venues of all shapes and sizes, from the pulsating dance floors of major nightclubs to the intimate cool vibes of smaller DJ bars. In 1990 all-night clubbing was legalized and everyone from hardcore party animals to quiet wallflowers just looking for a drink and conversation are catered for. Venues usually offer special rates in the early evening, but the real action starts later and continues until early morning.

Clubs

Bar Rumba
⊖ *Piccadilly. 36 Shaftesbury Ave, Piccadilly, W1V 7DD. 020 7287 6933. www.barrumbadisco.co.uk. Open Mon–Thu 10pm–3am, Fri–Sat 8pm–3am, Sun 9pm–3am.*
In the heart of Soho, the Rumba is one of London's best clubs even if the dance floor is far too small given the club's popularity. There's always a good atmosphere and the music varies from night to night, ranging from jazz, funk, house, drum n'bass to latino.

Borderline
⊖ *Tottenham Court Rd.Orange Yd, off Manette St, W1D 4JB. 020 7734 5547. www.mamacolive.com/ theborderline. Open Tue–Thu 11pm–3am, Fri–Sat 11pm–4am.*
An alternative vibe and a friendly crowd who love to dance fill this lively club nightly. The Saturday night Christmas Club indie night is London's longest running.

Cargo
⊖ *Old St. 83 Rivington St, EC2A 3AY. 020 7739 3440. www.cargo-london.com. Open Mon–Thu 6pm–1am, Fri–Sat 6pm–3am, Sun 6pm–midnight.*
Located in a Victorian railway arch, offering a restaurant, bar with lounge furnished with big cushions,

Cargo

and a heaving main room with a band. DJs offer great music from Asian underground to hip-hop.

Fabric
⊖Farringdon. 77a Charterhouse St, EC1M 3HN. 020 7336 8898. www.fabriclondon.com. Open Fri 10pm–5am, Sat 11pm–8am.
Opened in 1999, Fabric is a gigantic club capable of holding 1,500 revelers in three originally decorated halls. The acoustics are exceptional and attract top DJs and a mixed 20–30-year-old crowd. The music is predominantly drum n'bass and techno/house.

Heaven
⊖Charing Cross. Under The Arches, Villiers St, WC2N 6NG. 020 7930 2020. www.heaven-london.com. Open Mon, Wed, Thu, Fri–Sat 11pm–6am. Advance bookings.
Probably the world's most famous gay club is located under the railway arches near Charing Cross station. There are three dance floors and three types of music from disco to techno and a stunning laser show. The place is popular, but friendly.

Ministry of Sound
⊖Elephant & Castle. 103 Gaunt St, Elephant and Castle, SE1 6DP. 0870 0600 0101. www.ministry ofsound.com. Open Fri 10.30pm–6.30am, Sat 11pm–7am.
London's best-known nightclub has become an institution in the capital and draws a mixed, young crowd for house, garage, and techno music every weekend. The sound is exceptional but behave yourself if you want to get through the door, and above all be patient.

Cabaret at Madame Jojos

www.neolestat.com/Madame Jojo's

Cabaret

Circus
⊖Covent Garden. 27–29 Endell St, Soho, WC2H 9BA. 020 7420 9300. circus-london.co.uk. Open Tue–Wed 6pm–midnight, Thur 6pm–1am, Fri–Sat 6pm–2am.
Glamour and kitsch combine in this restaurant and bar cum circus venue. You never know what you might get here – acrobats, sword swallowers, burlesque – except that it will be high quality. The food is excellent too, and acts take place right above your heads or, if you're sitting on the long main table, on the table itself.

Madame Jojo's
⊖Piccadilly Circus. 8–10 Brewer St, Soho, W1R 3SP. 020 7734 3040. www.madamejojos.com. Usually open Tue–Wed & Fri–Sun, shows start at 7pm.
Focusing on Burlesque and variety, this warm-hearted cabaret for night owls is a favorite haunt of drag queens. Sometimes it can be a bit of a madhouse, but the ambience changes from day to day and it's never unfriendly.

NIGHTLIFE

121

SHOPPING

London's shops offer a wide range of goods to satisfy the most demanding shopper. There are many shopping areas in the city, with famous department stores, high street chains, or small specialist (and sometimes expensive!) boutiques found across town. In recent years large shopping malls have come to London, with the opening of Westfield's two sites: in Shepherd's Bush to the west and Stratford to the east.

Prêt-à-porter

If you've got designs on fashion, you're in the right place. Keep an eye out for classic garments, jewelry, and homeware from Jasper Conran. Check out the exclusive Burberry range, line up some of Sir Paul Smith's bright shirts and loud cufflinks, and head to H&M for the latest must-have high street fashions. Joseph's signature look—smart, tailored, and modern —and Vivienne Westwood's bold designs are worth a look too. To add the ultimate sparkle to your visit, head to the Hatton Garden jewelry shops.

Shopping streets

London's main shopping street is **Oxford Street★** *(see City of Westminster)*, with large department stores and high-street chains. Liberty, Hamleys, Aquascutum, and Jaeger all line **Regent Street★★**, while made-

to-measure clothing for men is available in **Savile Row** (tailors) and **Jermyn Street★** (shirt-makers) *(see City of Westminster)*. For trendy shops offering styles from established and offbeat designers, visit the **King's Road, Carnaby Street** (a high spot of the Swinging Sixties), and **Covent Garden**. The craft studios at **Oxo Tower** on the South Bank and **Camden Lock Market** are places to explore for a special gift.

Department stores

Fortnum & Mason

⊖ *Piccadilly Circus. 181 Piccadilly, W1A 1ER. 020 7734 8040. www. fortnumandmason.com. Open Mon–Sat 10am–9pm, Sun noon–6pm.* A gourmet paradise—their hampers are legendary. Also sells upmarket goods such as luggage, accessories, and cosmetics.

🍴 Harrods

⊖ *Knightsbridge. 87–135 Brompton Rd, Knightsbridge, SW1X 7XL. 020 7730 1234. www.harrods.com. Open Mon–Sat 10am–8pm, Sun 11.30am–6pm.* Harrods boasts that it can supply anything, even a pedigree dog. The food halls are particularly impressive. A world of elegance and comfort, to be visited as you would a museum.

Food hall, Harrods

©Harrods

Harvey Nichols
⊖ Knightsbridge. 109–125 Knightsbridge, SW1X 7RJ. 020 7235 5000. www.harveynichols. com. Open Mon–Sat 10am– 8pm, Sun 11.30am–6pm.

"Harvey Nicks" regularly raises eyebrows with its unusual and daring window displays. There's a good range of designer fashion clothing, a fabulous choice of hats (for Ascot!), and some fine jewelry.

John Lewis
⊖ Oxford Circus. 278–306 Oxford St, W1A 1EX. 020 7629 7711. www.johnlewis.com. Open Mon– Fri 9.30am– 8pm (Thu 9pm), Sat 9.30am–7pm, Sun 11.30am–6pm.

Suppliers of household fittings, linen, and stationery. This store has everything you need for everyday, practical purposes and is a beloved household name.

Hamley's Toy Shop, Regent Street
London's largest toy kingdom, Hamleys, has seven floors of wonders such as teddy bears, electric trains, and the very latest in electronic games.
⊖ Oxford Circus. 188–196 Regent St, W1B 5BT. 0870 333 2455. www.hamleys.com.

Liberty★★
⊖ Oxford Circus. 210–220 Regent St, W1R 6AH. 020 7734 1234. www.liberty.co.uk. Open Mon –Sat 10am–8pm, Sun noon–6pm.

An intimate and fabulous emporium of luxury design: Liberty-brand silks, Chinese ceramics, glassware, and designer clothes.

John Lewis, Oxford Street

Selfridges
⊖ Bond St. 400 Oxford St, W1A 1AB. 0870 837 7377. www.selfridges.com. Open Mon–Sat 9.30am–9pm, Sun 11.30am–6.15pm.

This well-known department store sells everything from lingerie to household articles, beauty products, fashion, and stationery.

SHOPPING

Malls

Westfield London

⊖Shepherds Bush; White City. Wood La, W12 7SL. 020 3371 2300. uk.westfield.com. Open Mon–Sat 10am–10pm, Sun noon–6pm.
Shopping mall giant Westfield's first UK venture opened in 2008 and has 265 shops (including a special premium luxury brands area, the Village), restaurants, bars, and a cinema.

Westfield Stratford City

⊖Stratford; Stratford International, W12 7SL. 020 8221 7300. uk.westfield.com. Open Mon–Fri 10am–9pm, Sat 9am–9pm, Sun noon–6pm.
This vast retail emporium opened at the Olympic Park in 2011 and is the largest urban shopping centre in the EU. It has some 300 stores, from high end to high street.

High street chains

French Connection

⊖Bond St. 396 Oxford St, W1C 7JX. 020 7629 7766. www.frenchconnection.com. Open Mon–Fri, 9.30am–9pm, Sat 9.30am–8pm, Sun 12.30–6pm.
Upscale high street fashion with good tailoring.

H&M

⊖Oxford Circus. 261–271 Regent St, W1B 2ES. 020 7493 4004. www.hm.com. Open Mon–Sat 10am–9pm, Sun noon–6pm.
Flagship UK store of trendy Swedish chain selling very moderately priced fashion and accessories for men, women, and children.

Karen Millen

⊖Oxford Circus. 229–247 Regent St, W1B 2EW. 020 7629 1901. www.karenmillen.com. Open Mon–Fri 10am–8pm (Thu 9pm), Sat 10am–7.30pm, Sun 11.30am–6.30pm.
British chain offering feminine, chic fashion and accessories. More expensive than high street.

Topshop

⊖Oxford Circus. 583–540 Oxford St, WC1D 1LA. 020 7499 0434. www.topshop.com. Open Mon–Sat 9am–9pm, Sun 11am–5pm.
Cheap, cheerful, and cutting edge, Topshop is an institution among fashionistas. The stock changes pretty much every week—key pieces featured in magazines sell out almost instantly.

Smaller shops

Burberry

⊖Bond St; Oxford Circus. 21–23 New Bond St, W1S 2RE. 020 7980 8425. www.burberry.com.
In 1997, the somewhat stodgy English brand was rejuvenated by a team of talented young designers. Classic and very British.

Foyles

⊖Tottenham Court Rd. 113–119 Charing Cross Rd, WC2H 0EB. 020 7437 5660. www.foyles.co.uk.
The world's greatest bookshop specializes in rare books while maintaining a comprehensive general list.

MUST DO

Gieves & Hawkes
⊖ *Piccadilly Circus. 1 Savile Row, W1S 3JR. 020 7434 2001. www.gievesandhawkes.com.*
On London's premier street for gentlemen's tailoring, this is the most famous outfitter of them all. Offers the classic British essentials.

Neal's Yard Dairy
⊖ *Covent Garden. 17 Shorts Gardens, WC2H 9AT. 020 7240 5700. www.nealsyarddairy.co.uk. Closed Sun.*
This popular cheese merchant sells fine dairy products from the British Isles only.

Penhaligon's
⊖ *Covent Garden. 41 Wellington St, WC2E 7BN. 020 7836 2150. www.penhaligons.com.*
Perfume supplier to the aristocracy since 1870, Penhaligon's counts the Royal Family among its clientele.

Philip Treacy
⊖ *Sloane Sq. 69 Elizabeth St, Belgravia, SW1W 9PJ. 020 7730 3992. Closed Sun.*
This master milliner is always in the public eye, at Ascot and in lifestyle and fashion magazines.

Vivienne Westwood
⊖ *Piccadilly Circus. 44 Conduit St, W1S 2LY. 020 7393 3900. www. viviennewestwood.com. Closed Sun.*
The lady known as "Queen Viv," who brought punk to a nation, continues to show off her talent and extravagance, including an exquisite eye for tailoring.

Jermyn Street★
A street with a distinctly masculine flavor in SW1. Shops include bootmakers, hatters, tailors, shirtmakers, shoemakers, and tobacco merchants. Floris the perfumer's, established in 1730, is at no. 89, and the noted purveyors of cheese and Scottish products, Paxton & Whitfield, at no. 93.

Auctioneers

Bonhams
⊖ *Knightsbridge. Montpelier St, SW7 1HH. 020 7393 3900. www.bonhams.com.*
Founded in 1793, Bonhams is the top vintage car valuers in Britain.

Christie's
⊖ *South Kensington. 8 King St, SW1Y 6QT. 020 7839 9060. www.christies.com.*
Founded in 1766, this internationally renowned institution built its reputation by promoting young artists such as Gainsborough.

Sotheby's
⊖ *Bond St. 34–35 New Bond St, W1A 2AA. 020 7293 5000. www.sothebys.com.*
Sotheby's started out in 1744 as a book valuers and launched Internet auctioning in 1999.

SHOPPING

MARKETS

Browsing market stalls holds a fascination for people in search of a bargain, antiques lovers hoping to find that desirable object, or those looking for a gift to take home. There are markets specializing in antiques, arts and crafts, vintage clothing, gourmet foods, and flowers and plants. The earlier you arrive, the greater the choice.

Alfie's Antiques Market
⊖ *Edgware Rd. 13–25 Church St, NW8 8DT. 020 7723 6066. www. alfiesantiques.com. Antiques & vintage. Open Tue–Sat 10am–6pm.* Don't be put off by its slightly scruffy appearance; this indoor market sells just about everything, but it's best to know what you're looking for.

Bermondsey Market
⊖ *Bermondsey; London Bridge. Bermondsey St, Southwark, SE1 4QB. 020 7525 6000. www. southwark.gov.uk. Antiques & bric-a-brac. Open Fri 6am–noon.* Trade in copper and silverware, Victorian jewelry, furniture, and objets d'art begins by torchlight in the early hours. The market attracts many dealers from around the local area, and is a mecca for serious collectors.

Berwick Street
⊖ *Tottenham Court Rd; Oxford Circus. Berwick St, Soho, W1. Fruit, veg, fabrics, clothes, household items. Open Mon–Sat 9am–6pm.* The market, dating from 1778, is one of the finest fresh produce markets in the city. Frequented by many local restaurateurs, it has an atmosphere of bygone times.

Borough Market
⊖ *London Bridge. Stoney St, Borough High St, Southwark, SE1 1TL. 020 7407 1002. www. boroughmarket.org.uk. Fresh food. Open Mon–Tue (lunch only) 10am–re5pm, Wed–Thu 10am–5pm, Fri 10am–6pm, Sat 8am–5pm.*

Borough Market

Alex Hare / age fotostock

This gourmand's paradise is probably the oldest food market in London. Known as "London's larder," it is respected for its organic products and mouth-watering fresh food stands.

Brick Lane Market
⊖Aldgate East. Brick La, E1. *Bric-a-brac, fabrics, clothes. Open Sun 8am–2pm.*
A vast chaotic hotchpotch of a market, from indian fabrics to cheap leather jackets, with plenty of junk in between.

Camden Markets
⊖Camden Town. Camden Town, NW1. www.camdenlock.net. *Open daily10am–6pm.*
There are three markets in Camden, all within a few minutes of each other. **Camden Market** (corner of Buck St and Camden High St; 020 7284 2084) is a treasure trove for bargain leather goods and clothing, with more than 200 stands. **Camden Lock Market** (Chalk Farm Rd, NW1 8AF; 020 7284 2084) has a wide range, from arts and crafts to stands selling multicultural food. **Stables Market** (Chalk Farm Rd, NW1 8AH; 020 7485 8355) is the place for alternative fashion, with 350 outlets selling everything from vintage clothing to antiques and period furniture. All the markets get mega-crowded at weekends.

Camden Passage
⊖Angel. Camden Passage, Islington, N1 5ED. 020 7359 0190. www.camdenpassageislington. co.uk.
Camden Passage, stretching over several streets, is full of antique shops. The antiques market (Wed, Sat, Sun) offers Oriental art, Art

Nouveau, Art Deco, silverware, and more from around 250 dealers.

Columbia Road Market
⊖Old St; buses 26, 48, 55. *Columbia Rd, Bethnal Green, E2. http://columbiaroad.info. Flowers, plants. Open Sun 8am–3pm.*
This popular flower market is a victim of its own success, but as well as the flowers, there are secondhand stores, chic boutiques, and a good bakery. The street has a village atmosphere, which lends it a certain charm.

Columbia Road Market

Grays Antiques Market & Grays in the Mews
⊖Bond St. 58 Davies St, W1K 5LP & 1–7 Davies Mews, W1K 5AB. 020 7629 7034. www.graysantiques. com. *Antiques. Open Mon–Fri 10am–6pm, Sat 11am–5pm.*
Occupying a split site incorporating the Mews, the main hall has 170 stands and London's biggest collection of antique jewelry.

Greenwich Market
⊖Cutty Sark. Greenwich High Rd, SE10. *Antiques & collectables (Thu–Fri), arts & crafts (Thu–Sun). Open Wed–Sun 10am–5.30pm.*

MARKETS

Covent Garden Market

The old flower market, haunted by the memory of Eliza Doolittle, now houses shops, cafés, restaurants, and wine bars. The Apple Market in the center and the Jubilee Hall Market on the south side of the Piazza both sell an unusual and imaginative range of goods. Mondays it's antiques and collectables. Tuesdays to Fridays the general market sells clothes, gifts, and handicrafts, while at the weekends the focus is arts and crafts.

⊖ *Covent Garden. 41 The Market, Covent Garden, WC2E 8RF. www.covent gardenlondonuk.com. Open Mon–Sat 10am–7pm, Sun 11am–6pm.*

Expect to find international crafts and collectables rather than real antiques here, but the atmosphere is pleasant and family-orientated.

Leadenhall Market
⊖ *Bank. Whittington Ave, EC3. 0871 789 6001. www.leadenhall market.co.uk. Fresh food. Open Mon–Fri 7am–4pm.*
A poultry and fish market housed in the huge and impressive Victorian Hall of Glass.

Leather Lane Market
⊖ *Chancery La. Leather La, EC1. Clothing & household goods. Open Mon–Fri 10.30am–2pm.*
The market, dotted with cafés, is always full of bargains. Fashionable clothes, sportswear, a tailor, but curiously, not much leatherwear.

Old Spitalfields Market★
⊖ *Liverpool St. Brushfield St, Commercial St, E1. www. spitalfields.co.uk. Fashion, arts & crafts. Open Mon–Fri 10am–5pm, Sat 11am–5pm, Sun 9am–5pm.*
This large historic hall is home to a craft market. On Thursdays, the secondhand stands display their wares, but on Sunday the organic food market is at its busiest. Pleasant atmosphere with plenty of shops, bars, and cafés.

Petticoat Lane Market
⊖ *Liverpool St. Middlesex St, Wentworth St, EC1. Open Sun 9am–2pm (Wentworth St also open Mon–Fri 10am–2.30pm).*
A daily flea market just down the road from its original 17C location; best on Sundays.

Portobello Road★
⊖ *Notting Hill Gate; Ladbroke Grove. Portobello Rd, Notting Hill, W11 1AN. 020 7229 8354. www. portobelloroad.co.uk. Antiques & bric-a-brac. Open Sat 8am–5pm.*
Browse for Victoriana, silver, chinaware, and postage stamps. Sited in trendy Notting Hill, so don't expect a bargain.

Portobello Road Market

Pawel Libera/Visit London

MUST DO

RESTAURANTS

The venues listed below were selected for their ambience, location, and/or value for money. Prices indicate the average cost of an appetizer, main course, and dessert for one person. Most restaurants open daily (except where indicated) and accept major credit cards. Tax and service are generally included in the restaurant bill. Tipping is optional, but it is common to leave 10% when the service is good. It is advisable to book in the evenings, particularly at weekends. Call or check website for information regarding reservations, dress code, and opening hours.

Luxury	**££££**	Over £75	*Moderate*	**££**	£25–£45
Expensive	**£££**	£45–£75	*Inexpensive*	**£**	Under £25

City of Westminster

Al Duca
£ Italian
⊖ *Piccadilly Circus. 4–5 Duke of York St, St James's, SW1Y 6LA. 020 7839 3090. www.alduca-restaurant. co.uk. Closed Sun.*
This Italian restaurant offers good value for money as well as a relaxed atmosphere.

Bali Bali
£ Indonesian
⊖ *Covent Garden. 150 Shaftesbury Ave, WC2H 8HL. 020 7836 2644. www.balibalirestaurant.com.*
Delicious, spicy Indonesian dishes and friendly service in a central location. Does pre-theatre menus.

Benihana
£ Japanese
⊖ *Piccadilly Circus. 37 Sackville St, W1S 3EH. 020 7494 2525. www.benihana.co.uk.*
Come here to marvel at the dexterity of the Japanese chefs as they cook the dishes right in front of you. Also at 77 Kings Road, Chelsea.

Carluccio's
£ Italian
⊖ *Covent Garden; Leicester Sq. Garrick St, WC2E 9BH. 020 7836 0990. www.carluccios.com.*
Well-priced chain of restaurants set up by Italian chef Antonio Carluccio. Relaxed ambience and airy, modern dining rooms make it

Benihana

©Paul Winch-Furness/Benihana

Modern dining at Carluccio's

©Carluccio's

a popular lunch spot. *Located all over London; check website for details.*

Chada Chada
£ Thai
⊖ *Bond St. 16–17 Picton Pl, Marylebone, W1M 5DE. 020 7622 2209. www.chadathai.com.*
Authentic and delicately spiced traditional Thai dishes as well as some surprises. Good service.

Jenny Lo's Tea House
£ Chinese
⊖ *Victoria. 14 Eccleston St, SW1W 9LT. 020 7259 0399. Closed Sat–Sun.*
There's an imaginative menu at this "canteen" style diner. Come early to avoid queues. Authentically Chinese. Cash only.

The Providores & Tapa Room
£ Spanish/Fusion
⊖ *Baker St. 109 Marylebone High St, W1U 4RX. 020 7935 6175. www.theprovidores.co.uk.*
Sit in the buzzing Tapa Room, open all day, for great breakfasts and tapas. Upstairs the restaurant serves fusion food, using unusual ingredients to great effect.

Rock and Sole Plaice
£ Fish
⊖ *Covent Garden. 47 Endell St, WC2H 9AJ. 020 7836 3785. www.rockandsoleplaice.com.*
This informal fish and chips eatery, founded in 1871, has portions big enough to satisfy all appetites, and somewhat kitsch aquatic decor.

Union Café
£ Mediterranean
⊖ *Bond St. 96 Marylebone Lane, Marylebone, W1U 2QA. 020 7486 4860. www.brinkleys.com/union cafe.asp.*
This laid-back restaurant is tucked away in a lane near the **Wallace Collection**. Open-plan kitchen and innovative cooking at fair prices.

🍴 Chain restaurants
For a budget-friendly meal try one of London's chain restaurants. Good value Italian staples are served at **Pizza Express** (www.pizzaexpress. com). For Asian cuisine head to **Wagamama** (www. wagamama.com) or try **Ping Pong** (www.pingpongdimsum. com) for dim sum. **Cote** (www. cote-restaurants.co.uk) serves affordable French fare.

MUST EAT

Villandry
£ French
⊖ *Great Portland St. 170 Great Portland St, Marylebone, W1W 5QB. 020 7631 3131. www. villandry.com. Closed Sun eve.*
Take a walk around the daytime deli before sampling the freshly prepared dishes in the restaurant to the rear. A relaxed, informal eatery with wooden tables.

Hunter 486
££ Brasserie
⊖ *Marble Arch. 50 Great Cumberland Pl, W1H 7FD. 020 7724 0486. www.thearchlondon.com.*
Superb steaks and a selection of fresh seafood served in an opulent yet cosy bar-brasserie with high-sided leather booths and an excellent, inventive cocktail list.

Mon Plaisir
££ French
⊖ *Covent Garden. 21 Monmouth St, Covent Garden, WC2H 9DD. 020 7836 7243. www.monplaisir. co.uk. Closed Sun.*
London's oldest French restaurant was founded more than 50 years ago, and has four dining rooms all decorated with a Gallic touch.

The Punch Bowl
££ British
⊖ *Bond St. 41 Farm St, London W1J 5RP. 020 7493 6841. www.punchbowllondon.com.*
Authentic, honest British cuisine served in an upmarket public house. Dishes are made with seasonal, locally sourced produce including meat from Mayfair's oldest butchers, Allens.

Rules
££ British
⊖ *Covent Garden. 35 Maiden La, Covent Garden, WC2E 7LB. 020 7836 5314. www.rules.co.uk.*
Grouse, partridge, and woodcock are some of the game on the menu at what is reputedly London's oldest restaurant – and all from its own estate! Antique cartoons adorn the walls.

The Ivy
£££ British
⊖ *Leicester Sq. 1 West St, Covent Garden, WC2H 9NQ. 020 7836 4751. www.the-ivy.co.uk.*
Once past the liveried doorman and waiting paparazzi, you'll find wood panelling, stained glass, and an unpretentious British menu. The Ivy is one of London's most coveted "Theaterland" restaurants, so securing a table is a challenge – call in late (about 10pm) for the best chance.

Royal China Club
£££ Chinese
⊖ *Baker St. 40-42 Baker St, W1U 7AJ. 020 7486 3898. http://www2.royalchinagroup.biz/.*
Top-notch Chinese cuisine including excellent Peking duck, lobster and abalone, served in an elegant dining room by ultra professional – and knowledgeable – staff. Ask them to match wines to your dishes, you won't be disappointed.

The Goring Dining Room
£££ British
⊖ *Victoria. Beeston Pl, SW1W 0JW. 020 7396 9000. www.thegoring.com.*
The Dining Room at this outstanding five-star hotel serves

the very finest British cuisine. Lit by chandeliers and attended by the most professional wait staff in town, this is a dining experience not to be missed. Start with a drink in the old-school lounge-style bar and don't leave without sampling the delights of the cheese trolley.

The Greenhouse
££££   French
⊖ Green Pk. 27A Hay's Mews, W1J 5NY. 020 7499 3331. www. greenhouserestaurant.co.uk.
Book a table at Arnaud Bignon's restaurant for one of the best meals of your life. The six-course tasting menu changes with the seasons but always features the very best French gastronomy, with a twist of originality.

The Square
££££   French
⊖ Bond Street. 6-10 Bruton St, W1J 6PU. 020 7495 7100. www.squarerestaurant.com.
Philip Howard's world-class restaurant serves haute cuisine with a flourish of cutting-edge creativity. Dinner here is a real treat, with the tasting menu providing a line-up of mouthwatering dishes matched with well-chosen wines. This stalwart of the London dining scene has been at the top of the tree for decades for a reason.

City of London

1 Lombard Street (Brasserie)
££   Modern European
⊖ Bank. 1 Lombard St, EC3V 9AA. 020 7929 6611. www.1lombard street.com. Closed Sat, Sun.
A former banking hall provides the grand setting for this brasserie. A popular venue for City workers and often quite noisy.

Le Coq d'Argent
££   Modern European
⊖ Bank. No. 1 Poultry, EC2R 8EJ. 020 7395 5000. www.coqdargent. co.uk. Closed Sat lunch, Sun eve.
This spectacular, sophisticated restaurant on top of one of the City's modern buildings also boasts a terrace. The crustacea bar is terrific.

Le Coq d'Argent

D&D restaurants

White Swan Pub & Dining Room
££   British
⊖ Chancery La. 108 Fetter La, EC4A 1ES. 020 7242 9696. www.thewhiteswanlondon.com. Closed Sat–Sun.
Choose from a traditional pub menu downstairs or the award-winning fine dining room upstairs.

Kensington, Chelsea, and Knightsbridge

L'Accento
£   Italian
⊖ Bayswater. 16 Garway Rd, Bayswater, W2 4NH. 020 7243 2201, www.laccentorestaurant.co.uk. Closed Sun.

A favorite with aficionados of authentic Italian provincial cuisine, with delicious shellfish specialties.

The Churchill Arms
£ Thai
⊖*Notting Hill Gate. 119 Kensington Church Street, W8 7LN. 020 7727 4242, churchillarmskensington.co.uk.*
Mouthwatering (and spicy!) Thai food served in a fine traditional pub with real ale on tap.

No 11 Pimlico Road
£ Modern European
⊖*Sloane Sq. 11 Pimlico Rd, SW1W 8NA. 020 7730 6784. www.theebury.co.uk.*
A posh gastropub, with an elegant upstairs dining room serving accomplished cooking using seasonal ingredients.

Island Restaurant and Bar
£ Modern European
⊖*Lancaster Gate. Lancaster Terrace, W2 2TY. 020 7551 6070. www.islandrestaurant.co.uk.*
There are great views of Hyde Park through the long windows of this airy restaurant, and good modern European cooking as well.

Itsu
£ Japanese
⊖*South Kensington. 118 Draycott Ave, Chelsea, SW3 3AE. 020 7590 2400. www.itsu.com. No bookings.*
Take your pick of the European-style sushi as it passes along the conveyor belt. Dishes are priced according to color, and help is just a buzzer call away. Now also a chain of fast food shops across London, ideal for a quick lunch.

Kam Tong
£ Chinese
⊖*Bayswater. 59–63 Queensway, Bayswater, W2 4QH. 020 7229 6065, www.kamtong.org.uk.*
This long-established Chinese restaurant offers a cheaper menu than many in the area. Bow-tied waiters supervise the dim sum.

Malabar
£ Indian
⊖*Notting Hill Gate. 27 Uxbridge St, Kensington, W8 7TQ. 020 7727 8800. www.malabar-restaurant.co.uk.*
Lovers of Indian food flock to this restaurant. Choose from an extensive range of good-value dishes, and many vegetarian options.

Shikara
£ Indian
⊖*South Kensington. 21 Bute St, SW7 3EY. 020 7581 6555. www.shikara.co.uk.*
Pretty restaurant serving excellent Indian food at good prices in a usually expensive neighborhood.

Aubaine
££ French
⊖*South Kensington. 260–262 Brompton Rd, SW3 2AS. 020 7052 0100. www.aubaine.co.uk.*
The place for summer when the windows roll back. Good bakery at the front, and imaginative food. Friendly, with large tables.

Belvedere
££ French
⊖*Kensington Olympia. Holland House (off Abbotsbury Rd), Kensington, W8 6LU. 020 7602 1238. www.belvedererestaurant.co.uk.*

On a summer's day secure a table on the balcony terrace of this 19C orangery in the middle of Holland Park. The menu offers a modern take on classic French dishes.

Bibendum Oyster Bar
££ Fish
⊖ *South Kensington. 81 Fulham Rd, SW3 6RD. 020 7589 1480. www.bibendum.co.uk.*
The foyer of London's beloved Art Nouveau gem, Michelin House, provides the setting for an informal meal of light seafood and shellfish specialties. Like many Conran eateries, it's usually packed.

Momo
££ Moroccan
⊖ *Piccadilly Circus. 25 Heddon St, W1B 4BH. 020 7434 4040, www. momoresto.com. Closed Sun lunch.*
The "in" crowd love this colorful restaurant, with its traditional rugs and atmospheric Arabic music. Staff will guide the uninitiated through the menu.

Racine
££ French
⊖ *Knightsbridge. 239 Brompton Rd, SW3 2EP. 020 7584 4477, www.racine-restaurant.com.*
Dark leather banquettes and large mirrors create a Parisian brasserie atmosphere. The cooking is far superior, however, offering regional and classic French dishes.

Scott's
££ Seafood
⊖ *Bond St. 20 Mount St, W1K 2HE. 020 7495 7309. www.scotts-restaurant.com.*
Founded in 1851 and a favorite haunt of Winston Churchill, Scott's was given a face lift in the 1990s.

The upstairs room specializes in oysters and fish dishes, with snacks in the piano bar downstairs.

Bluebird
£££ Modern European
⊖ *South Kensington. 350 King's Rd, SW3 5UU. 020 7559 1000. www.bluebird-restaurant.com.*
Sir Terence Conran's Chelsea "gastrodome" comprises foodshop, flower market, café, dining room, and the Bluebird, a skylit restaurant and bar. The weekend brunch is always popular.

Bluebird restaurant and bar

©Bluebird Cafe/D&D London

Zafferano
£££ Italian
⊖ *Knightsbridge. 15 Lowndes St, Belgravia, SW1X 9EY. 020 7235 5800. www.zafferanorestaurant.com.*
Book weeks in advance to secure a table at one of London's finest Italian restaurants. Enjoy robust dishes that reflect the season and save a space for the wonderful tiramisu.

MUST EAT

Sophisticated dining at Nobu

©Paul Winch-Furness/Nobu

Gordon Ramsay
££££ French haute cuisine
⊖ Sloane Sq. 68–69 Royal
Hospital Rd, SW3 4HP. 020 7352
4441. www.gordonramsay.com/
royalhospitalroad.
Getting a table at the exclusive
signature restaurant of this celebrity
chef is a challenge, and it's best
to start at least two months in
advance. The reward is fabulous
food and top flight service.

Nobu
££££ Japanese
⊖ Green Park. 19 Old Park La,
W1K 1LB. 020 7447 4747.
www.noburestaurants.com.
Booking essential.
At the Metropolitan's ultra-trendy
eatery, the creative cuisine attracts
a celebrity clientele. Minimalist
decor. Come with a large wallet.

South Bank and Southwark

The Fire Station
£ Mediterranean
⊖ Waterloo. 150 Waterloo Rd,
South Bank, SE1 8SB. 020 7620
2226, www.thefirestation
waterloo.com.

Located between the Old Vic
and Waterloo Station, this
1910 fire station specializes in
Mediterranean cuisine. Tiled
floor, church pews, and an open
kitchen contribute.

Fish!
£ Seafood
⊖ London Bridge. Cathedral St,
Borough Market, Southwark,
SE1 9AL. 020 7407 3803.
www.fishkitchen.com.
Inside this modern glass and
metal structure you can choose the
fish as well as the cooking method
and accompanying sauce.

Gillray's
££ British
⊖ Waterloo. County Hall,
Westminster Bridge Rd. 020 7902
8000. gillrays.com
Only the very best Aberdeen Angus
beef makes it through the door
of this top notch steak restaurant.
Enjoy views of the London Eye and
Big Ben from the large windows
and settle in for one of the best
steaks of your life served with truffle
chips and portobello mushrooms.
Excellent selection of gins too – so
start with a G&T.

RESTAURANTS

Oxo Tower Brasserie
£££ Modern European

⊖ *Southwark. Barge House St (8th floor), Oxo Tower Wharf, Southwark, SE1 9PH. 020 7803 3888. www.harveynichols.com.*
Sharing the eighth floor of a converted factory with a formal restaurant, the brasserie offers terrace dining and the same great views.

Tower Hill, Greenwich, and East London

Café Naz
£ Indian

⊖ *Aldgate East. 46–48 Brick La, E1 6RF. 020 7247 0234. www.cafenaz.co.uk.*
Brick Lane is renowned for its Indian restaurants, and Café Naz is a contemporary take on the theme with Bangladeshi specialties.

Foxcroft & Ginger
£ British

⊖ *Whitechapel. 69-89 Mile End Rd, E1 4TT. foxcroftandginger.co.uk*
One of London's best brunch venues – strong coffees, perfectly poached eggs and homemade sourdough bread served by friendly staff in a funky, glass-fronted building. Pizzas are served in the evenings (from 5pm) and you won't be able to resist the amazing line-up of cakes along the counter!

Café Spice Namasté
£ Indian

⊖ *Tower Hill. 16 Prescot St, Whitechapel, E1 8AZ. 020 7488 9242. www.cafespice.co.uk. Closed Sat lunch, Sun.*
A riot of color with a friendly atmosphere and fragrant, competitively priced food.

North Pole Piano Restaurant
£ Modern European

⊖ *New Cross. 131 Greenwich High Rd, Greenwich, SE10 8JA. 020 8853 3020. www.northpole greenwich.com.*
This lively, trendy establishment, just a short stroll from the center of Greenwich, has two bars and an upstairs restaurant serving good food in a casual atmosphere.

Blueprint Café
££ Modern European

⊖ *Bermondsey. Design Museum, Butler's Wharf, Bermondsey, SE1 2YD. 020 7378 7031. www.blue printcafe.co.uk. Closed Sun eve.*
After visiting the Design Museum, secure a window table in this adjoining airy, modern restaurant and enjoy the views of Tower Bridge, the City, and Docklands.

Hoxton Grill
££ American

⊖ *Old St. 81 Great Eastern St, EC2A 3HU. 020 7739 9111, www.hoxtongrill.com*
Relax on the comfortable banquette seating in this ultra stylish brasserie-style restaurant

---

Pie and eels

You'll get a real taste of old London at Manze's eel, pie and mash shop, which has been serving locals since 1902. The decor in this family-run business is beautiful and the welcome is warm.
⊖ *Tower Hill. 87 Tower Bridge Rd, SE1 4TW. 020 7407 2985. www.manze.co.uk.*

---

and order chargrilled steaks, cooked to perfection. The chateaubriand is particularly good and the desserts are a tempting bunch – try the raspberry sundae or banoffee pie.

Boundary Restaurant
£££ French
⊖ *Shoreditch High St. 2–4 Boundary St, E2 7DD. 020 7729 1051. www.theboundary.co.uk*
Stunning French cooking which lets the high quality of the premium ingredients used shine through. Start with the chariot de charcuterie before feasting on Cornish lobster or Perigord truffles. Great wine list too (largely French) and the decor is all opulence.

Bloomsbury, Camden, and Islington

Abeno
£ Japanese
⊖ *Holborn. 47 Museum St, WC1A 1LY. 020 7405 3211. www.abeno.co.uk.*
An original Japanese restaurant near the British Museum. Try the delicious house specialty, Okonomi-yaki, pancakes cooked on a hotplate at your table.

Camden Brasserie
£ Modern European
⊖ *Camden Town. 9–11 Jamestown Rd, Camden, NW1. 020 7482 2114. www.camden brasserie.co.uk.*
For over 20 years this popular brasserie has provided the perfect lunch spot after a morning at the market. Specialties include grilled fish and meats.

North Sea Fish Restaurant
£ Fish
⊖ *Russell Sq. 7–8 Leigh St, WC1H 9EW. 020 7387 5892, www.north seafishsrestaurant.co.uk. Closed Sun.*
Drop in to this friendly eatery for genuine fish and chips. Only ground nut or vegetable oil is used and egg and matzo coating also available. Jumbo sizes fried or grilled.

The Queens
£ British
⊖ *Chalk Farm. 49 Regent's Park Rd, Primrose Hill, NW1 8XD. 020 7586 0408. www.youngs.co.uk.*
One of London's "gastropubs," the Queens serves hearty traditional British dishes. Grab a seat on the balcony overlooking Primrose Hill.

St John
£ British
⊖ *Farringdon. 26 St. John St, Islington, EC1M 4AY. 020 7251 0848. www.stjohnrestaurant.com. Closed Sat lunch, Sun eve.*
This busy, unpretentious restaurant is housed in a 19C smokehouse. The bar is a popular with the after- work crowd, while the menu focuses offal and a mix of traditional and rediscovered British dishes.

St John

Laurie Fletcher/St. John Restaurant Ltd

Olivelli
£ Italian

⊖Goode St. 35 Store St, WC1E 7BS. 020 7255 2554. www.pizza paradiso.co.uk. Closed Sun.

Founded in 1934, this pizzeria-ristorante with its typical decor of assorted bottles and black and white photos has retained much of its original atmosphere and serves good pizza.

Outer London

Banners
£ International

⊖Finsbury Park. 21 Park Rd, Crouch End, N8 8TE. 020 8348 2930, www.bannersrestaurant.com.

Trendy restaurant with a lively atmosphere serving a varied menu of world cuisine and daily specials. Good breakfast menu.

Light House
£ Italian & fusion

⊖Wimbledon. 75–77 Ridgeway, Wimbledon, SW19 4ST. 020 8944 6338, www.lighthousewimbledon. com. Closed Sun eve.

Close to Wimbledon station, this bright restaurant has an open kitchen and a changing menu of Italian and fusion dishes.

Ma Cuisine
£ French

⊖Kew Gardens. 9 Station Approach, Kew, TW9 3QB. 020 8332 1923. www.macuisinebistrot.co.uk.

This real French "bistro" is a café by day and in the evenings serves the likes of boudin noir and cassoulet.

River Café
£ Italian

⊖Hammersmith. Rainville Rd, Thames Wharf, Hammersmith, W6 9HA. 020 7386 4200. www.river cafe.co.uk. Closed Sun eve.

This restaurant, housed in a converted warehouse, has young staff, an open kitchen, and first-rate Italian cuisine incorporating the best ingredients around.

The Glasshouse
££ Modern European

⊖Kew Gardens. 14 Station Parade, Kew, TW9 3PZ. 020 8940 6777. www.glasshouserestaurant.co.uk.

Adjacent to Kew Gardens Underground station, this Michelin one-star restaurant has a glass façade, a refined atmosphere, and very good service.

The Wells
££ French

⊖Hampstead. 30 Well Walk, Hampstead NW3 1BX. 020 7794 3785. www.thewellshampstead. co.uk.

Attractive 18C pub on the edge of the Hampstead Heath, with plenty of leather armchairs to sink into after a ramble. The upstairs dining room offers classic French cooking, served with charm.

MUST EAT

LIGHT BITES

Cafés and informal eating places that keep flexible hours can provide a light meal in the middle of the day, or a snack at any time. An average meal in these places will cost under £15. The following café/restaurant chains have numerous branches throughout Central London and provide consistent value for casual meals: Pret A Manger, Eat, Caffè Uno, Café Rouge, Itsu, Chez Gérard, Wagamama, and Giraffe. Church refectories are another good place for light meals; those at Southwark Cathedral and St Martin-in-the-Fields are particularly notable.

Light Bites

Café Bohème
⊖ *Leicester Sq. 13–17 Old Compton St, W1D 5JQ. 020 7734 0623. www.cafeboheme.co.uk.*
A friendly place for a snack or a light meal, located in the very heart of Soho. The small bar gets very busy at weekends when there is also live jazz.

Café in the Crypt
⊖ *Charing Cross. Duncannon St, St Martin-in-the-Fields, WC2N 4JJ. 020 7766 1158. www.stmartin-in-the-fields.org.*
The self-service café installed in the lovely 18C vaulted crypt is one of the best places in the area for a quick, inexpensive snack; all proceeds go to the famous church.

De Gustibus
⊖ *Bond St. 53 Blandford St, W1H 3AF. 020 7486 6608. www.degustibus.co.uk. Closed Sat–Sun.*
This award-winning shop boasts an extensive range of freshly baked breads with Mediterranean-influenced fillings and other enticing snack food. Eat in the brightly decorated café, on the pavement terrace, or take away.

Harvey Nichols Fifth Floor Café & Champagne Bar
⊖ *Knightsbridge. 109–125 Knightsbridge, SW1X 7RJ. 020 7823 1839. www.harveynichols.com.*
Well-heeled shoppers enjoy a glass of champagne or a pot of tea in the informal atmosphere of an airy café-bar, with a roof terrace that overlooks Knightsbridge.

Harvey Nichols, Fifth Floor Champagne Bar

© Harvey Nichols

The Knightsbridge Café
⊖ *Knightsbridge. 5–6 William St, Knightsbridge, SW1X 9HL. 020 7235 4040.*
Just a credit card's throw from Knightsbridge's designer shops, a café with smart modern decor, slick service, and a wide range of salads, sandwiches, and pastries. Attractive pavement terrace. Open for breakfast, lunch, and dinner.

139

Konditor & Cook
◯London Bridge. 10 Stoney St, SE1 9AD. 020 7407 5100. www.konditorandcook.com.
One of the great café/delis in the foodie paradise Borough Market, it buzzes all day with people buying takeaways or stopping for a coffee and a piece of cake.

Mo'Café
◯Piccadilly Circus. 25 Heddon St, W1B 4BH. 020 7434 4040. www.momoresto.com.
Mo, the small relaxed café adjoining Mourad Mazouz's Moroccan restaurant, invites you to North Africa, with all the trappings, such as an alfresco terrace with low souk style seating, mint tea, and sweet honey pastries.

Ottolenghi
◯Notting Hill Gate. 63 Ledbury Rd, W11 2AD. 020 7727 1121. www.ottolenghi.co.uk.
This café, deli, and restaurant, which serves a mix of fashionable dishes with lots of Asian spices, is a great hangout for all the trendy "Notting Hillbillies."

Paul
◯Covent Garden. 29 Bedford St, WC2E 9ED. 020 7836 3304. www.paul-uk.com.
Crusty bread, wonderful pastries, and great lunchtime snacks are on offer in this delightful—and very French—bakery.

Raoul's
◯Warwick Ave. 13 Clifton Rd, Maida Vale, W9 1SZ. 020 7289 7313. www.raoulsgourmet.com.
Great at the weekend, this smart café/deli with outside seating is the place for classic dishes like croque monsieur and good coffee.

Southwark Cathedral Refectory
◯Southwark. Southwark Cathedral, SE1 9DA. 020 7407 5470, cathedral.southwark.anglican.org.
Good hearty fare such as soups, stir-frys, and pasta dishes that are reasonably priced.

New Tom's
◯Notting Hill. 226 Westbourne Grove, Notting Hill, W11 2RH. 020 7221 8818.
Owned by the son of Sir Terence Conran, this half-deli, half-café is a popular spot with the fashionable Notting Hill crowd.

Delicious display at Ottolenghi

©Keiko Oikawa/Ottolenghi

AFTERNOON TEA

This celebrated institution is offered in tea rooms, cafés, and hotels all over the city. The traditional time for tea is 4pm, but most establishments serve it between 3pm and 5pm. Order a selection of sandwiches—cucumber is traditional—or a cream tea (scones, jam, and clotted cream) or crumpets, English muffins, cakes, and pastries, and choose your tea with care—Darjeeling, Lapsang Souchong, or the refined Earl Grey.

Browns Hotel
⊖ Green Park. 33–34 Albermarle St, W1S 4BP. 020 7493 6020. www.roccofortehotels.com.
Enjoy an excellent afternoon tea in the wonderful setting of this delightfully traditional, elegant hotel.

Fortnum & Mason
⊖ Piccadilly Circus. 181 Piccadilly, W1A 1ER . 020 7734 8040. www.fortnumandmason.com.
You can take tea in any of the five restaurants, but the fourth-floor St James's Restaurant is the most popular for a real afternoon feast.

Harrods
⊖ Knightsbridge. Brompton Rd, Knightsbridge, SW1X 7XL. 020 7730 1234. www.harrods.com.
London's most famous emporium presents an array of restaurants and cafés to suit all palates. For a traditional tea, make for the fourth-floor Georgian Restaurant.

The Landmark London
⊖ Bond St. 222 Marylebone Rd, NW1 6JQ. 020 7631 8000. www.landmarklondon.co.uk.
Take tea under the glass roof in the lovely winter garden of this traditional hotel. On Sundays, brunch is served to the sounds of live jazz.

The Lanesborough
⊖ Hyde Park Corner. Hyde Park Corner, SW1X 7TA. 020 7259 5599. www.lanesborough.com.
Taking tea in "The Conservatory" by the plants and fountain is a must for all lovers of tradition.

The Orangery
⊖ Kensington High St. Kensington Palace Gdns, W8 3UY. 0844 482 7777. www.hrp.org.uk.
This delightful 18C orangery in the grounds of Kensington Palace is the ideal spot for afternoon tea.

The Ritz
⊖ Green Park. 150 Piccadilly, W1V 9DG . 020 7493 8181. www.theritzlondon.com.
Served in the spectacular Palm Court, taking tea at this legendary hotel is an institution. Jacket and tie—and booking—required.

Palm Court, The Ritz

©Ritz Hotel London

PUBS

Pubs' opening hours are usually Mon–Sat 11am–11pm and Sun noon–10.30pm. Many larger pubs have later licenses up to midnight or even 1am. Gastropubs offer a variety of dishes from fish and chips to Asian cuisine. In more traditional pubs, you can still find classic British dishes, such as steak and ale pie, sausages, and puddings. The traditional drink is beer, sold in pints and half pints, bottled or draft. A freehouse sells whatever beers it chooses. If the house is tied, it will sell the product of its brewery owner. Of course wines, spirits, and soft drinks are always available, too.

City of Westminster

The Audley
J. Strachan/MICHELIN

The Audley
⊖ Bond St. 41 Mount St, Mayfair, W1K 2RX. 020 7499 1843.
This typical old Victorian gin palace with a grandiose paneled interior counts First Lady Michelle Obama among its clientele.

The Coal Hole
⊖ Temple; Charing Cross. 91–92 Strand, WC2R 0DW. 020 7379 9883.
This popular haunt, built in 1904, has a medieval-style decor and stone flag floors. Lively ambience and a clientele largely composed of office workers and tourists.

Cock Tavern
⊖ Blackfriars. 22 Fleet St, EC4Y 1AA . 020 7353 8570. Closed Sun.
"Ye Olde Cock Tavern" is 17C in style, with a paneled bar counter.

The Devereux
⊖ Temple. 20 Devereux Court, Essex St, Strand, WC2R 3JJ. 020 7583 4562. Closed Sat–Sun.
One of the best pubs in the area, with a flower-decked façade, excellent beer, and a restaurant. Always packed at peak times.

Golden Lion
⊖ Green Park; Piccadilly Circus. 25 King St, SW1Y 6QY. 020 7925 0007. Closed Sun.
This early 18C pub was the annexe of St James's Theatre before its demolition. It has preserved many features such as black marble pillars and a glass and mahogany interior.

Cock Tavern
Gwen Cannon/MICHELIN

142

The Guinea
⊖ *Bond St; Green Park.*
30 Bruton Pl, W1J 6NR. 020 7409
1728. Closed Sat lunch, Sun.
A small, welcoming pub with an old-fashioned charm, and a grill restaurant in the back room.

The Lamb & Flag
⊖ *Covent Garden. 33 Rose St,*
WC2E 9EB. 020 7497 9504.
This pub, nestling in a tiny alley, is the oldest and perhaps the most pleasant in the area. Good beer best enjoyed during off-peak hours.

Punch Tavern
⊖ *Blackfriars. 99 Fleet St, EC4Y*
1DE. 020 7353 6658. Closed Sun.
The drawings decorating the walls reflect that this was the birthplace of *Punch*, the celebrated satirical magazine. Excellent beer.

The Sherlock Holmes
⊖ *Embankment; Charing Cross.*
10–11 Northumberland St,
WC2N 5DA. 020 7930 2644.
A homage to the eponymous fictional detective, this pub boasts a reconstruction of his study with a host of associated objects. Less touristy than you might think.

Ye Olde Cheshire Cheese
⊖ *Blackfriars. 145 Fleet St,*
EC4A 2BU. 020 7353 6170.
A huge labyrinthine 17C pub with small beamed rooms and coal fires. A Fleet Street institution.

City of London

Black Friar
⊖ *Blackfriars. 174 Queen Victoria*
St, EC4V 4EG. 020 7236 5474.

Founded in 1875, London's only Art Nouveau pub, with stained glass, paintings, and sculptures.

Cittie of York
⊖ *Chancery La. 22–23 High*
Holborn, WC1V 6BS. 020 7242
7670. Closed Sun.
This 17C inn is truly unique. A pleasant room at the front and a church-like hall at the back, complete with "confessionals."

Jamaica Wine House
⊖ *Bank. St Michael's Alley,*
off Cornhill, EC3V 9DS. 020 7929
6972. Closed Sat–Sun.
A delightful watering hole with historical associations, hidden away in a small alley.

Lamb Tavern
⊖ *Monument. 10–12 Leadenhall*
Market, EC3V 1LR. 020 7626 2454.
Closed Sat–Sun.
The oldest pub in Leadenhall Market, the Lamb has stunning marble pillars and a glass roof. The terrace is busy at lunchtime.

The Seven Stars
⊖ *Chancery La. 53 Carey St,*
WC2A 2JB. 020 7242 8521.
A really charming pub dating from 1602. Lawyer, musician, and young student clientele.

Ye Olde Mitre
⊖ *Chancery La. 1 Ely Court,*
EC1N 6SJ. 020 7405 4751.
Closed Sat–Sun.
This historic, picturesque 16C pub with its irregular shaped rooms was once part of a bishop's residence.

Ye Olde Wine Shades
⊖ *Monument. 6 Martin La, EC4A*
2BU. 020 7626 6303. Closed Sat–Sun.

This delightful old pub (1663), with its dark wooden booths, serves excellent wines and a variety of bar snacks in the evenings.

Kensington, Chelsea, and Knightsbridge

Admiral Codrington
⊖ South Kensington. 17 Glossop St, SW3 2LY. 020 7581 0005.
This much-loved local is packed in the evenings. The dining area at the back has a retractable glass roof.

Dining room, Admiral Codrington

©The Admiral Codrington

The Bunch of Grapes
⊖ Knightsbridge. 207 Brompton Rd, Knightsbridge, SW3 1LA. 020 7589 4944.
This Victorian pub has all the hallmarks—a mahogany interior, engraved glass, and a wrought-iron balcony. A popular tourist spot.

Chelsea Potter
⊖ Sloane Sq. 119 King's Rd, SW3 4PL. 020 7352 9479.
Located in the heart of one of London's foremost shopping areas, this pub is authentic and unpretentious. Full of tourists by day and a young crowd at night.

Chelsea Ram
⊖ Fulham Broadway. 32 Burnaby St, SW10 0PL. 020 7351 4008.
A short walk from the King's Road, this friendly pub is very pleasant

with its scrubbed pine tables and walls packed with books and art.

Churchill Arms
⊖ Notting Hill Gate. 119 Kensington Church St, W8 7LN. 020 7727 4242.
An eclectic collection of Churchill memorabilia adorns this large cozy pub. Thai cuisine is served under the veranda in a jungle setting.

The Nag's Head
⊖ Knightsbridge; Hyde Park Corner. 53 Kinnerton St, Knightsbridge, SW1X 8ED. 020 7235 1135.
A country setting just five minutes from Harrods. As friendly a welcome as you'll receive anywhere in London.

The Westbourne
⊖ Royal Oak; Notting Hill Gate. 101 Westbourne Park Villas, Notting Hill, W2 5ED. 020 7221 1332.
Well renovated, with large windows and terrace, the Westbourne is very popular with locals.

South Bank and Southwark

The Anchor
⊖ London Bridge. 34 Park St, Bankside, SE1 9EF. 020 7407 1577.
This 18C tavern is associated with Shakespeare, Dr Johnson, and Samuel Pepys. Large riverside patio with great views.

Anchor & Hope
⊖ Waterloo; Southwark. 36 The Cut, SE1 8LP. 020 7928 9898. Closed Sun eve.
Crowds of people squeeze into this great pub, which has a real buzz. Along with all the chatter, you'll get excellent food that has won awards.

MUST EAT

BAR

Tower Hill, Greenwich, and East London

Cutty Sark Tavern
Greenwich. DLR Cutty Sark.
4–6 Ballast Quay, Lassell St,
SE10 9PD. 020 8858 3146.
Built in 1804, this tavern was a
meeting place for fishermen.
A charming, picturesque pub
with fine Thames views from
the terrace.

The Gun
DLR: Blackwall. 27 Coldharbour,
E14 9NS. 020 7515 5222.
This pub overlooking the Thames
is named after the neighboring
foundry that produced cannons
for Nelson's ships.

Prospect of Whitby
Wapping. 57 Wapping Wall,
E1W 3SP. 020 7481 1095.
Built in 1520, sailors would drink
here before sailing to the New
World. With a balcony terrace
beside the Thames, the pub is a
victim of its own success, packed
with coach-loads of tourists.

Town of Ramsgate
Wapping. 62 Wapping High St,
E1W 2PN. 020 7481 8000.
This historic pub sits by Execution
Dock, where the bodies of executed
pirates and thieves (Captain Kidd in
1701) were left for the tide to wash
over them three times.

Trafalgar Tavern
DLR: Cutty Sark, Greenwich. Park
Row, SE10 9NW. 020 8858 2909.
A delightful, but busy 19C pub with
bar food and restaurant, renowned
for its whitebait dinners.

Ghost story
According to the landlord, the
ghost of one of the Duke of
Wellington's officers can be
seen wandering around the
Grenadier and down the nearby
alley (one of London's most
picturesque). Friendly and cozy
pub with upmarket clientele.
Knightsbridge; Hyde Park
Corner. 18 Wilton Row, Belgravia,
SW1X 7NR. 020 7235 3074.

Bloomsbury, Camden, and Islington

The Camden Arms
Camden Town. 1 Randolph St,
Camden, NW1 0SS. 020 7267 9829.
Trendy lounge and gastropub
serving good Thai food. Excellent
array of potent cocktails and music
provided by guest DJs.

The Eagle
Farringdon; Chancery La.
159 Farringdon Rd, EC1R 3AL.
020 7837 1353.
One of London's first gastropubs,
the regular clientele enjoy a menu
of simple cuisine and a lively buzz.

Outer London

Crooked Billet
Wimbledon. 14 Crooked Billet
Rd, SW19 4RQ. 020 8946 4942.
A country- pub feel, with oak
beams, an open fire, real ales, and a
supposedly haunted cellar!

Dog & Fox
Wimbledon. 24 High St,
SW19 5DX. 020 8946 6565.
Landmark pub in Wimbledon
Village, close to the All England
Lawn Tennis and Croquet Club.

BAR

PUBS

The Dove
🚇 Ravenscourt Park. *19 Upper Mall, W6 9TA. 020 8748 9474.*
This former 18C coffee house, where the words of Rule Britannia are said to have been written, claims to have the smallest bar in the country.

The Flask
🚇 Highgate. *14 Flask Walk, Hampstead, NW3 1HE. 020 7435 4580.*
A quaint pub with a roaring fire in winter and a large terrace in summer. Karl Marx was once a frequent visitor. Good pub food, including Sunday roasts.

The Flask Tavern
🚇 Highgate; Archway. *77 Highgate West Hill, N6 6BU. 020 8348 7346.*
Delightful, historic pub with a warren of rooms, an outside courtyard, and decent pub grub.

London Apprentice
Rail: Syon La from Waterloo. 62 Church St, Isleworth, TW7 6BG. 020 8560 1915.
This attractive pub is named after the City livery company apprentices who stopped here for refreshment after their long row upstream.

The Rutland Arms
🚇 Ravenscourt Park; Hammersmith. *15 Lower Mall, W6 9DJ. 020 8748 5586.*
This Victorian pub has an attractive riverside location and is a traditional vantage point from which to watch the annual Oxford and Cambridge **Boat Race** *(see p 105).*

Spaniard's Inn
🚇 Hampstead. *Spaniards Rd, NW3 7JJ. 020 8731 6571.*
This tavern, founded in 1585, has many historic associations. Worth a trip out in summer.

HOTELS

London is an expensive place to stay and finding a suitable room in a city with over 27 million visitors a year, and an average hotel occupancy rate of 80%, often requires patience. The establishments listed below have been selected for their ambience, location, and/or value for money. Prices reflect the average cost for a standard double room for two people in high season. Breakfast is usually included. Bear in mind that advance reservation is a must in any season, especially over Christmas, Easter, and summer.

Luxury	**££££** Over £250	*Moderate*	**££** £115–£180
Expensive	**£££** £180–£250	*Inexpensive*	**£** £115 or less

City of Westminster

Luna Simone Hotel
£ 36 rooms
⊖ Pimlico. 47–49 Belgrave Rd,
SW1V 2BB. 020 7834 5897.
www.lunasimonehotel.com.
A family-run hotel with a warm welcome, vibrantly decorated bedrooms with thoughtful extras, and a well-equipped computer room.

Melbourne House Hotel
£ 17 rooms
⊖ Pimlico. 79 Belgrave Rd,
Victoria, SW1V 2BG. 020 7828 3516.
www.melbournehousehotel.co.uk.
A family-run hotel located a short walk from Tate Britain. Most of the simple but immaculate bedrooms have en suite shower rooms.

Melita House Hotel
£ 22 rooms
⊖ Pimlico. 35 Charlwood St,
SW1V 2DU. 020 7828 0471.
www.melitahotel.com.
In a fairly quiet residential street off Belgrave Road, Melita House offers spacious, modern rooms with fridges.

The Fielding
££ 24 rooms
⊖ Covent Garden. 4 Broad Court,
Bow St, Soho WC2B 5QZ. 020 7836 8305. www.the-fielding-hotel.co.uk.
A hotel enjoying an unrivaled location in a quiet pedestrian street in Covent Garden. Bedrooms are compact but well kept. A rare find for the area.

Blandford Hotel
££ 34 rooms
⊖ Baker St. 80 Chiltern St,
W1U 5AF. 020 7486 3103.
www.capricornhotels.co.uk.
Close to Regent's Park, this privately owned hotel has a friendly atmosphere, well-kept rooms, and an adjacent car park.

Durrants Hotel
££ 92 rooms
⊖ Bond St. 26–32 George St,
Marylebone, W1H 5BJ. 020 7935 8131. www.durrantshotel.co.uk.
This elegant hotel is quintessentially English. Enjoy afternoon tea in the fire-lit lounges or British fare in the wood-paneled dining room.

Hart House
££ 15 rooms

⊖ *Marble Arch. 51 Gloucester Pl, Marylebone, W1U 8JF. 020 7935 2288. www.harthouse.co.uk.*
This Georgian house that once provided refuge to French nobility fleeing the Revolution is now a welcoming well-maintained hotel.

Sanctuary House Hotel & Pub
££ 34 rooms

⊖ *St James's Park. 33 Tothill St, Westminster, SW1H 9LA. 020 7799 4044. www.fullershotels.com.*
A Victorian hotel above a pub offering good value rooms close to Big Ben and the London Eye.

Flemings
£££ 119 rooms

⊖ *Green Park. 7–12 Half Moon St, W1J 7BH. 020 7499 2964. www.flemings-mayfair.co.uk.*
Close to Green Park, the Georgian architecture of this traditional hotel is complemented with oil paintings and antique furniture.

Hazlitt's
£££ 23 rooms

⊖ *Tottenham Court Rd. 6 Frith St, Soho, W1D 3JA. 020 7434 1771. www.hazlittshotel.com.*
Virtually the only hotel in Soho, the former home of the eponymous essayist attracts a mix of well-heeled urban travelers. Plenty of Victorian charm.

St Martins Lane
£££ 200 rooms

⊖ *Charing Cross. 45 St Martin's La, Covent Garden, WC2N 4HX. 020 7300 5500. www.stmartins lane.com.*
Designed by Philippe Starck, this is one of London's most spectacular designer hotels: from state-of-the-art bedrooms to stylish bars and restaurants.

The Cavendish
££££ 295 rooms

⊖ *Piccadilly Circus. 81 Jermyn St, SW1Y 6JF. 020 7930 2111. www.thecavendish-london.co.uk.*
Opposite Fortnum & Mason, this large corporate hotel offers all the conveniences of a modern hotel.

🛎 Claridge's
££££ 143 rooms

⊖ *Bond St. Brook St, W1K 4HR. 020 7629 8860. www.claridges.co.uk.*
Playing host to stars, statesmen, and the royalty of Europe, Claridge's epitomizes English grandeur and is celebrated for its Art Deco design and luxury.

🛎 The Goring Hotel
££££ 69 rooms

⊖ *Victoria. 15 Beeston Pl, Grosvenor Gdns, Victoria, SW1W 0JW. 020 7396 9000. www.thegoring.com.*
Simply the best service in London. Five-star hotels don't get better than this stunning landmark hotel that has been in the Goring family for four generations. The elegant,

Dining room at the Goring
©The Goring, London

The Cavendish

©The Cavendish, London

spacious rooms have silk walls, opulent marble bathrooms and state-of-the-art lighting and music systems. Every detail has been considered – and is oh so English.

The Metropolitan
££££ 152 rooms
⊖ *Green Park. Old Park La, W1K 1LB. 020 7447 1000. www.comohotels.com/ metropolitanlondon.*
The favored haunt of celebrities, the Met offers ultra-minimalist design and views of Hyde Park from rooms on the upper floors.

City of London

Travelodge
£ 142 rooms
⊖ *Aldgate. 1 Harrow Pl, E1 7DB. www.travelodge.co.uk.*
Accommodation for the budget-conscious in the financial district. The en suite rooms are spacious and modern.

Kensington, Chelsea, and Knightsbridge

Amsterdam Hotel
£ 19 rooms
⊖ *Earl's Court. 7–9 Trebovir Rd, Earl's Court, SW5 9LS. 020 7370 5084. www.amsterdam-hotel.co.uk.*

This small hotel has rooms with vivid color schemes and some with balconies. In summer take advantage of the small garden.

Columbia Hotel
£ 103 rooms
⊖ *Lancaster Gate. 95–99 Lancaster Gate, Bayswater, W2 3NS. 020 7402 0021. www.columbia hotel.co.uk.*
Housed in a row of 19C houses, the room decor is unremarkable, but half overlook Kensington Gardens and many have balconies.

Garden Court Hotel
£ 32 rooms
⊖ *Bayswater. 30–31 Kensington Gardens Sq, W2 4BG. 020 7229 2553. www.gardencourthotel.co.uk.*
A friendly, family-owned hotel with a cozy lounge and simply furnished rooms, half of which are en suite. Good value.

Henley House
£ 21 rooms
⊖ *Earl's Court. 30 Barkston Gdns, Earl's Court, SW5 0EN. 020 7370 4111. www.henley househotel.com.*
Nestling in a pleasant square near the South Kensington museums, this small friendly hotel has well-priced, reliable accommodation.

HOTELS

Merlyn Court Hotel
£ 20 rooms
⊖ *Earl's Court. 2 Barkston Gdns, SW5 0EN. 020 7370 1640. www.merlyncourthotel.com.*
A friendly, family-run hotel with simple, comfortable rooms, some of which overlook a tranquil square.

Pavilion Hotel
£ 30 rooms
⊖ *Paddington. 34–36 Sussex Gdns, W2 1UL. 020 7262 0905. www.pavilionhoteluk.com.*
A quirky, intimate Victorian house brimming with bric-a-brac. Choose from a range of themed rooms.

Abbey Court
££ 22 rooms
⊖ *Notting Hill Gate. 20 Pembridge Gdns, W2 4DU. 020 7221 7518. www.abbeycourthotel.co.uk.*
An ideal base for antique hunters roaming Portobello Road, this elegant town house has a very personal touch and friendly staff.

Byron Hotel
££ 45 rooms
⊖ *Bayswater. 36–38 Queens-borough Terr, W2 3SH. 020 7243 0987. www.byronhotel.co.uk.*
Reasonably priced accommodation in the heart of Bayswater. Rooms are bright and spacious and all have en suite showers.

The Diplomat
££ 26 rooms
⊖ *Sloane Sq. 2 Chesham St, Belgravia, SW1X 8DT. 020 7235 1544. www.thediplomathotel.co.uk.*
A good value, imposing hotel in the heart of Belgravia with large, well-decorated rooms, all en suite.

Knightsbridge Hotel
£££ 44 rooms
⊖ *Knightsbridge. 10 Beaufort Gdns, Knightsbridge, SW3 1PT. 020 7584 6300. www.firmdale hotels.com.*
A porticoed town house tucked away behind Knightsbridge. The rooms vary in size but all have minibars and safes.

Knightsbridge Green
£££ 16 rooms
⊖ *Knightsbridge. 159 Knightsbridge, SW1X 7PD. 020 7584 6274. www.knightsbridge greenhotel.com.*
Discreet small hotel in the heart of the famous shopping district. Spacious rooms and reasonable rates for central London.

Miller's Residence
£££ 8 rooms
⊖ *Bayswater. 111a Westbourne Grove, Bayswater, W2 4UW. 020 7243 1024. www.millersuk.com.*
Amid the Bayswater shops, this quirky Victorian house is laden with fine antiques and has lavishly furnished bedrooms.

On a budget
The **Meininger Hostel**, owned by a German chain, provides functional, comfortable, stylish, and well-priced accommodation in dormitory, twin, or single rooms. Great location. ⊖ *South Kensington. 65–67 Queen's Gate. SW7 5JS. 020 7590 6190. www. meininger-hostels.com. 30 rooms.*

MUST STAY

Mandarin Oriental gardens

Portobello Hotel

£££ 24 rooms

⊖ *Holland Park. 22 Stanley Gdns, North Kensington, W11 2NG. 020 7727 2777. www.portobello-hotel.co.uk.*

An elegant white 19c terrace town house with rooms offering theatrical flourishes such as circular beds and deep free-standing Victorian bathtubs.

The Berkeley

££££ 186 rooms

⊖ *Knightsbridge. Wilton Pl, Knightsbridge, SW1X 7RL. 020 7235 6000. www.the-berkeley.co.uk.*

The Berkeley's discreet charm is evident in the paneled drawing room, rooftop pool with retracting roof, and opulent rooms.

Draycott House Hotel

££££ 35 rooms

⊖ *Sloane Sq. 26 Cadogan Gdns, Knightsbridge, SW3 2RP. 020 7730 6466. www.draycott hotel.com.*

Country house living minutes away from Harrods. This charming Victorian house has luxurious rooms, many of which overlook a tranquil garden. Room service.

Mandarin Oriental

££££ 65 rooms

⊖ *Knightsbridge. 66 Knightsbridge, SW1X 7LA. 020 7235 2000. www.mandarin oriental.com.*

Right in the heart of Knightsbridge, opposite Harvey Nichols, this luxury hotel lives up to its location

Rooftop pool at the Berkeley

HOTELS

with plush amenities and service to match. The Mandarin Bar is a favorite haunt of London's rich, famous, or wannabes.

South Bank and Southwark

Premier Inn London County Hall
££ 313 rooms
⊖ *Waterloo. Belvedere Rd, Waterloo, SE1 7PB. 0870 238 3300.*
www.premierinn.com.
Once home to the Greater London Council, this hotel offers spotless, uniformly fitted rooms.

Park Plaza Westminster Bridge
£££ 1,019 rooms
⊖ *Waterloo. 200 Westminster Bridge Rd, SE1 7UT. 0870 238 3300.*
www.parkplaza.com.
This sleek, upmarket hotel has thoroughly modern rooms with state-of-the-art facilities and a spacious feel. The riverside location is unbeatable (there are views of Big Ben from some rooms) and service is impeccable. Relax in the 15-metre swimming pool or have a treatment in the Mandara Spa.

Tower Hill, Greenwich, and East London

Holiday Inn Express London Greenwich
££ 70 rooms
⊖ *Greenwich. Bugsby Way, SE10 0GD. 020 8269 5000.*
www.hiexpress.co.uk.
This seven-story modern hotel, just south of the O2 Arena, has great panoramic views and a Chinese restaurant.

Hoxton Hotel
£–£££ 208 rooms
⊖ *Old St. 81 Great Eastern St, EC2A 3HU. 020 7550 1000.*
www.hoxtonhotels.com.
This trendy hotel in the heart of Shoreditch attracts a funky crowd to its uber-cool rooms, with their leather walls, sleek black bathrooms and sumptuous beds. Some rooms have views of the Shard, all have a modern desk space, flatscreen TV and free wifi – plus books almost everywhere you look. Breakfast is delivered to the room and there's fresh milk for tea.

The Boundary
££££ 17 rooms
⊖ *Shoreditch High St. 2-4 Boundary St, Shoreditch E2 7DD. 020 7729 1051.*
www.theboundary.co.uk.
The Boundary is surely the best designed hotel in London. Every room is individually designed by Terence Conran and features bespoke furniture with real wow factor. Sleep soundly on the very best mattress, bedding and linens and soak in the bath, before heading upstairs to the Rooftop for cocktails overlooking Shoreditch. Rooms have Apple TV, iPod docking stations and flatscreen TVs.

Bloomsbury, Camden, and Islington

Hotel Cavendish
£ 33 rooms
⊖ *Goodge St. 75 Gower St, WC1E 6HJ. 020 7636 9079.*
www.hotelcavendish.com

DH Lawrence once stayed at this Georgian house, run by the same family for over 40 years. Period furniture adds to the charm.

Crescent Hotel
£ 27 rooms
⊖ *Russell Sq. 49–50 Cartwright Gdns, WC1H 9EL. 020 7387 1515. www.crescenthoteloflondon.com.*
A charming hotel with a loyal clientele. Boasts a cozy sitting room, large garden, and tennis courts.

Gresham Hotel
£ 40 rooms
⊖ *Tottenham Court Rd. 36 Bloomsbury St, WC1B 3QJ. 020 7580 4232 . www.the-gresham -london.co.uk.*
Guests at this Georgian house benefit from competitive prices and a location near the Underground station. Not all rooms are en suite.

Thanet Hotel
£ 16 rooms
⊖ *Russell Sq. 8 Bedford Pl, WC1B 5JA. 020 7636 2869. www.thanethotel.co.uk.*
Housed in a Georgian terrace, the personable owners create a relaxing and friendly ambience.

Academy Hotel
££ 49 rooms
⊖ *Goodge St. 21 Gower St, WC1E 6HG. 020 7631 4115. www.theacademyhotel.co.uk.*
The Georgian exterior belies the contemporary interior of this "boutique" hotel. Rooms are stylish and comfortable. Bar and restaurant.

Grange Blooms Hotel
££ 26 rooms
⊖ *Russell Sq. 7 Montague St, WC1B 5BP. 020 7323 1717. www.grangehotels.com.*
Housed in a row of Georgian houses flanking the British Museum, Blooms is charming and intimate. Individually designed "themed" rooms and a small rear garden.

Malmaison
£££ 97 rooms
⊖ *Farringdon. Charterhouse Sq, EC1M. 020 7012 3700. www.malmaison-london.com.*
Charming and elegant, this hotel is set on a cobblestone square close to Smithfield market. The decor is chic, and there's a gym, brasserie restaurant, and rooftop bar.

The Rookery
£££ 32 rooms
⊖ *Farringdon. 12 Peter's La, Cowcross St, Islington, EC1M 6DS. 020 7336 0931. www.rookery.co.uk.*
This charming restored 18C house, with wood-paneling, period furniture, and open fires, is located near St Paul's Cathedral. Bathrooms have Victorian fittings.

Charlotte Street
££££ 44 rooms
⊖ *Tottenham Court Rd; Goodge St. 15 Charlotte St, W1T 1RJ. 020 7806 2000. www.firmdalehotels.com.*
A contemporary English hotel renowned for its charm. Individually appointed rooms and a stylish bar and restaurant. Well located on the Bloomsbury fringes.

HOTELS

Outer London

Chase Lodge
£ 13 rooms
National Rail Services from Waterloo, Vauxhall, Clapham Junction and Wimbledon to Hampton Wick. 10 Park Rd, Hampton Wick, KT1 4AS.020 8943 1862. www.chaselodgehotel.com.
A warm welcome is guaranteed at this Victorian property located a short distance from the Thames. Comfortable, individual rooms.

Hampstead Village Guesthouse
£ 9 rooms
Hampstead. 2 Kemplay Rd, Hampstead, NW3 1SY. 020 7435 8679. www.hampsteadguest house.com.
A Victorian house, close to Hampstead Heath. Not all rooms are en suite, but all are decorated with antiques.

Langorf Hotel
£ 36 rooms
Finchley Rd. 18–20 Frognal, Hampstead, NW3 6AG. 020 7794 4483. www.langorfhotel.com.
An Edwardian house with a breakfast room, a walled garden, spacious rooms, and convenient transport links to central London.

Mountview
£ 3 rooms
Finsbury Park. 31 Mount View Rd, N4 4SS. 020 8340 9222. www.mountviewguesthouse.com.
An attractively furnished Victorian house in a quiet residential tree-lined street. Bedrooms are individually decorated and two overlook the rear garden.

London Heathrow Marriott
££ 393 rooms
Heathrow Terminals 1, 2, 3. Bath Rd, Hayes UB3 5AN. 020 8990 1100. www.marriott.com.
Top pick of the hotels at Heathrow airport, this modern four-star has spacious comfortable rooms with high quality bedding and contemporary bathrooms. Eat in the intimate Italian restaurant, quaff champagne in the stylish lobby bar and swim in the lovely heated indoor pool.

MUST STAY

LONDON

Churches, cinemas, galleries, and museums are listed under **bold headings**. For complete lists of cafés, hotels, markets, pubs, restaurants, shops, and theaters, see the Must Do, Must Eat, and Must Stay sections. Those listed under the bold headings are also mentioned in the main text.

INDEX